Dear Tricia,

Peace Lies
Within

May peace fill your heart
♡

Love, Stella
x

Peace Lies Within

108 ways to tame your mind and connect to inner peace

Stella Tomlinson

Contents

Introduction   1

Get out of your head   17

Breathe here now   55

Make friends with your emotions   83

Shift your perspective   119

Open your heart   165

Create connection   199

What next?   250

I recommend   251

Acknowledgements   253

About the author   254

Introduction

Hi there. I'm Stella, and I have a busy mind.

I have a creative mind; an anxious mind; a judgmental mind; an imaginative mind; a worried mind; an angry mind; a complex, multi-faceted, amazing and annoying mind.

In short, I have a human mind.

You do too.

How would you describe your relationship with your mind?

I used to feel at the mercy of my mind.

The way it jumps around here and there. The way it can get stuck in a rut of ruminating and fretting over the same thing, day in and day out. The way it never seems to shut up and give me a moment of peace!

As you're reading this, chances are you feel something similar?

Yes? You, me and the vast majority of the human population: lost in thought!

Ah, the human mind. It's such a powerful tool.

Capable of such amazing feats of imagination and creation: works of art; plays and poems; scientific discoveries; complex projects and planning; courage and bravery; and simple acts of kindness.

But this capacity for imagination and creation all too easily turns inwards on itself. Jumping here and there, imagining the worst and creating all sorts of mischief in the process.

It flits around and judges. Wanting this, not wanting that. Pulling and pushing.

All too often never quite satisfied with what we have or what we're experiencing in the here and now.

It's all rather tiring isn't it? And it certainly gets in the way of any connection to feeling a sense of inner peace.

The mind pulls us out of this moment and stops us enjoying the people we are with, or the quiet-time we're allowing ourselves, or the simple pleasures of the sights and sounds around us that can bring us joy and enrich our lives.

Throughout my life and hearing from and observing others whether they be family, friends, colleagues or my yoga and meditation students, I have come to the conclusion that so much of the stress we experience is down to what appears to be going on between our ears: our minds.

The types of thoughts we think and the way they keep running on a loop contribute to feeling stressed, and this makes our body stressed, and when the body feels stressed our mind picks up on it and we end up in a downward spiral of negativity and disempowerment.

The capacity for feeling peaceful and present and content and connected to everything around us is something we're born with. No new-born baby is worrying about the future — other than when the next feed is coming! Young children are naturally spontaneous.

But at some point, we become disconnected from this natural, peaceful state of play and presence.

Up until the age of seven, the brain of young human beings is like a sponge — taking everything in as literal truth without a filter. Around the age of seven, major changes occur in the brain; the frontal and temporal lobes put on the biggest growth spurt of any time in our lives. These lobes are the parts of the brain that control cognitive functions, and they also are making neural connections with the system that controls emotions. In other words, thinking and emotions come online. At this stage, you could say the human mind gets a major overhaul.

Then as we grow up and move into adulthood — through the years of schooling, exams and peer-interaction/pressure — we receive millions of messages from teachers, carers, friends, family and people in positions of authority and the media. These messages programme our minds, telling us how to act, what to look like, what to value, and even who we should be.

Add to this mix our individual life experiences, innate and learned preferences, and our expectations and goals which may or may not correspond to the external messages about life and success we've received over the years.

All of this gives our mind a lot to make sense of and assimilate, in turn creating the potential for inner conflict as the mind compares and analyses and judges.

The mind is often at the core of our struggles. And this struggle leads us to forget our true nature and obscures the natural state of relaxation and inner peace and wisdom and joy that we are born with.

But it is possible to find peace with your mind. You'll probably never make it completely quiet (not while you're conscious anyway!). But you CAN find a greater sense of acceptance and freedom.

And this is why I've written this book.

To help you understand your mind and tame it, so you no longer feel at the mercy of its wanderings and criticisms and the sheer noise of all the thoughts scrabbling for your attention. To help you see that peace lies within and you have the means to reconnect to it.

Because this is what I have needed over the years. And the practices and perspectives I share with you in this book are those that I have learned and used to tame my mind and to deeply feel and experience that there is another, more peaceful, way to live.

What I share in this book offers paths to greater self-understanding, self-acceptance, self-compassion, and inner peace and joy.

Now don't get me wrong.

Your mind is not your enemy.

It's not something you need to defend yourself against. It's not something to be scared of or to defeat or control.

Your mind can be your greatest friend and support.

It just needs taming!

When you tame your mind, you can harness its power to create and connect and understand and empathise. And live life with a greater sense of ease and inner peace.

So, what is this thing we call the mind? Let's take a look.

What is the mind?

It's worth taking a few moments to stop and consider; what is this mind that can be amazing and infuriating at the same time?

Where is it? What is it? Is it in the brain or somewhere else?

Now, nobody has the definitive answer to this one, so I'm not going to pretend I do.

One way of looking at it is this:

OK, so we have a brain; that physical organ we all know we have within our heads. It's the one apparently in charge. A central unit processing everything we're experiencing and telling the rest of the body what to do.

The mind can be seen as something the brain does. Some would say the mind is the product of the brain and is located within it.

In this sense, the mind is 'a set of cognitive faculties including consciousness, perception, thinking, judgement, language and memory. It is usually defined as the faculty of an entity's thoughts and consciousness. It holds the power of imagination, recognition, and appreciation, and is responsible for processing feelings and emotions, resulting in attitudes and actions.' {Wikipedia}

This point of view says the brain is the thing that translates the content of your mind — your thoughts, feelings, attitudes, beliefs, memories and imagination — into electrical activity and chemical releases that we experience as emotions and feelings.

However, there are other more esoteric and philosophical ways of looking at this. Another perspective is that there is just one realm of being, of which consciousness and matter are part, but they are one and the same and can't be separated. Our brain tunes into this realm and filters our experience of it through the senses and our lived experience and what comes through that filter is what we experience as our thoughts - our mind.

Hmm, confused yet? (Writing that last paragraph gave *me* brain ache!)

So, for the purposes of this book, I'd like to settle on a sense that the human mind is awareness; a consciousness that is aware of itself and what is going on around it. We'll let the scientists and philosophers and mystics continue their age-old argument about the detail.

What follows is not a definitive way of looking at this. You may disagree. Or it might get you thinking about it, and in doing so give your mind a job for a while (which is an important element of mind taming).

Anyway, this conscious awareness might be filled with thoughts. Or it might be fully in tune with the present.

But it's the same basic thing.

Let's work with that! Our mind can experience serenity and stillness and connection and oneness. But most of the time that is not what we're experiencing. It's more like mayhem and movement and disconnection and confusion.

Now part of this is down to the fact that the brain has an inherent negativity bias. It's programmed to scan; to roam; to wander; to look out for danger. It's programmed to keep us alive. And this leads to the mind creating ways to keep us safe.

Trouble is, when there's no immediate danger to attend to the mind wanders off into ruminating on the past, or flits off to worrying about the future.

And these perceived 'threats' set off our stress response as if our lives depended on it; just as if worrying about going to the dentist or that funny look a colleague gave you are real threats to your life. And the thoughts we generate about ourselves, such as not feeling good enough or loveable, produce the same stress response.

Put shortly; much of our stress and inner conflict and fear and doubt is caused by our mind.

And we need to add something else into this mix; emotions. Emotions are energy in motion within us; those physical sensations we feel in our body that arise from the circumstances we're experiencing and the thoughts we're thinking.

Strong emotions also contribute to a feeling that we're at the mercy of our inner landscape — and strong challenging emotions such as anger, fear and doubt are very much felt by the body and contribute to feelings of stress.

So, let's take a look at stress and why it's something we must be aware of and address in our lives.

When you learn to tame your mind and reconnect to inner peace, you vastly reduce your stress levels!

The effects of stress

Let me put it plainly. If you're always at the mercy of your mind, thoughts and beliefs about yourself and the world, which causes your body to be constantly operating in stress-response mode, then you **will** become ill.

Take it from me, I know (I wound up with stress, migraines, anxiety and irritable bowel syndrome).

When you are in continual stress-mode, your immune system is suppressed, your digestive system runs poorly, and your muscles are in a constant state of hyper-vigilance getting ready to fight, run or freeze in the presence of danger.

When you're in stress-mode your levels of cortisol are constantly raised in your body, and this disrupts all of the body's major processes and systems and can lead to:

- depression
- fatigue
- weight gain
- back pain

- decreased concentration
- low libido
- impaired memory (especially short-term)
- insomnia
- skin complaints and poor skin healing
- irritability
- menstrual abnormalities
- blood sugar dysregulation/high blood sugar
- decreased bone mineral density
- high blood pressure.

Blimey. That's quite a list.

I don't mean to scare you.

Scrap that. I DO mean to scare you! #sorrynotsorry
It's time to wake up.

And to do something about it.

Looking after your mind and emotions IS VITAL to your physical, mental and spiritual wellbeing (if I could put this in flashing lights, I would!).

Tending to your mind and emotions is not selfish, it's an act of love and is self-less because in caring for yourself you will have more energy, presence and compassion to show up and be there for your friends, family, and colleagues.

Because if you're running on empty and drained, stressed and ill, you are no use to anyone!

And, you're not honouring this precious human life you have been gifted.

I love the wisdom of Buddha on this:

'*To keep the body in good health is a duty ... otherwise we shall not be able to keep our mind strong and clear.*'

So, lecture over.

Do you get it?

Learn to tame your mind and reconnect to inner peace.

Reduce your stress: for the good of yourself; your family and friends; and the whole of humanity!

What is inner peace?

Now it's also worth taking a few moments to reflect on what inner peace means.

Of course, what it means to you may be very different to what it means to me, so it's worth contemplating this.

Take some time now — what does inner peace mean to you?

Words and ideas like these may arise: calm, content, quiet, still, ease, switching off, focus, thinking positive thoughts, feeling positive, emotional stability, resilience, accepting, relaxed, tranquil, serene, blissful, joyful, self-possessed; I'm sure you can add some more.

Inner peace can be seen as freedom from the effects of stress — a state that can be maintained even in the face of challenges and stressors.

And, significantly, these are all descriptions of inner states of being.

Inner peace, by its very nature, is found within yourself. You won't find it searching around in the material world around you, or relying on other people to provide it.

Yes, our environment, our work and finances and our relationships do of course feed into how we feel within ourselves.

But, ultimately, how we feel inside ourselves is ours alone to own and direct. It is your decision how you deal with what's going on in your life and the wider world. It is your decision if, and how, you choose to create meaningful connection in your life.

Truth! An uncomfortable one maybe, but still the truth.

Living from a place of inner peace is not passive; it's not about accepting harmful behaviour or letting yourself get pushed around, or wandering around with rose-tinted spectacles pretending all is well and denying life's challenges.

I feel it's actually rather radical.

It's about choosing to take responsibility.

It's choosing to be courageous and take ownership of your feelings and thoughts.

It's choosing to be honest with yourself.

It's choosing not to react or let your buttons get pushed so, you no longer lash out and cause pain and confusion around you.

It's choosing to act and live with awareness of the consequences of your thoughts, words and actions.

It's choosing to show up in your life as a complex and amazing human being.

Taming your mind and choosing to live in connection with inner peace is not necessarily easy, but neither does it have to be complicated.

The first step in this practice is intention; deciding that you want to live in a different way; accepting the truth that peace does, in fact, lie within you (rather than looking for it externally) and that you believe you can connect to it.

That's the first step to allow the magic to unfold.

But please be aware that it's not a linear journey from A to B.

Living from a place of inner peace takes courage and resilience: and practice.

And this book aims to offer you some ways to practise.

How to use this book

With this book I wish to inspire you to become present; to shift your perspective to let go of limiting beliefs; find emotional balance; accept and care for yourself, and look within. So you can rediscover the inner peace, which is your birth right, together with contentment and radiance and joy, so you can live from this place eternally.

Each section contains inspirations, insights, actions and practices.

Some are very down to earth and practical; some are tools; some are perspectives; some are poetic and inspiring.

Over my years of practice and teaching, I have concluded there are six steps to taming the mind and connecting to inner peace. See them as six keys to unlock the peace that lies within:

Get out of your head: I offer you practices and perspectives to enable you to feel more grounded; to get out of your head and into your body. To bring you out of the past, and back from the future, into the here and now. These are the foundations of taming your mind to connect to inner peace.

Breathe here now: with this section, I share simple, effective and powerful techniques and perspectives to help you to harness the power of your breath; to tame your mind and your body's stress response; to feel more in control, settled and calm.

Make friends with your emotions: next, I share perspectives and practices to empower you to change your relationship with your emotional landscape; to make friends with your emotions so you can feel more peaceful, aware and balanced.

Shift your perspective: here I'm sharing guidance and practices that aim to shift your way of thinking. To empower you to realise that you are not at the mercy of events, challenges, other people; or your mind.

Open your heart: in this section, I offer you guidance and tools to open your heart and to be kinder to yourself. To soften and open and allow. Your emotional and spiritual heart is your inner wellspring of peace.

Create connection: and finally, I aim to empower you to bring a sense of connection back into your life through simple actions and perspective shifts; to create a renewed sense of meaning in your life; to strengthen the connections you already have, and to put peace into action.

You could read the book from cover to cover, but you might find it more useful to use it like an oracle and open up to intuitive guidance. Ask a question and open at a random page and trust that the guidance you need is contained within that passage.

Keep the book by your side. Dip into it daily.

Take the practices and use them.

Ponder on different perspectives to open your mind to a different way of being.

Live the contents of this book; don't just passively consume it. Bookmark the things that resonate with you most and take action!

Each passage ends with a 'Mind Taming Peace Mantra' – summing up the piece in a sentence. A sentence you can take as a mantra — a chosen thought — and repeat to yourself, write on post-it notes, or meditate on it to help you to tame your mind and feel more peaceful.

Why me?

For the past near-on 20 years, I have been on a journey to tame my mind and connect to inner peace.

Before and during this journey I've experienced intense stress and anxiety, and have experienced the sweaty palms, dodgy digestion, chronic tension and lack of sleep that can come with it.

I've lacked confidence and not loved myself nor trusted my intuition; not even hearing it — blocking it out through lack of self-trust — and that busy mind!

But I've discovered that there is another way of being. There is a place within me and also within you that exists beyond the busy mind. A place of peace and calm and connection. This place is your natural self: peaceful, strong, resilient and wise. It's who you were before your busy mind took control. And it's who you still are once you learn to tame your pesky mind and put it back in its place as the servant, not the master!

My journey to writing this book began in around 2000 when I first experienced yoga, not long after I'd moved to a new city where I knew no-one, for my first professional job in a large organisation. I felt tense, anxious, self-conscious and seriously stiff and inflexible. Yoga stretched and relaxed my body and helped me to find peace with my mind and offered a pathway to navigate the demands, stresses and busyness of life.

13

The practices I share in this book have come from this journey of practice, study and exploration. They have helped me to transform my relationship with myself and transform my life, and they continue to provide me with the means to move from stress to peace, from tension to relaxation, from confusion to clarity and from self-judgment to self-acceptance and love.

And I know they will help you too.

Why? Because they're based on ancient wisdom and modern science.

I am a qualified Dru Yoga and Meditation teacher and have studied the peace-bringing, awakening teachings and practices of yoga, meditation and mindfulness since the year 2000. I've also learned about some of the modern knowledge regarding the brain and nervous system; what goes on in our bodies when we're stressed; the power of intention and the effects of thoughts and emotions on our bodies and inner chemistry, and how this interacts with the world around us.

What I share with you in this book is what I have studied, learned, taught and — mostly importantly — practised over the years.

Why 108 ways?

Why? Because 108 has long been considered a sacred number in yoga.

There are 108 beads on a mala, which is the string of beads often used as an aid in meditation (and I meditate daily to check in with myself and connect to inner peace).

There are numerous explanations for the significance of this number, but the one that resonates most deeply with me is this: within your body and energy systems therein, there are said to be 108 pathways to your heart.

My wish for you

And with the 108 passages contained within this book, my dearest wish is that they each offer you a pathway to **your** heart.

Pathways to self-acceptance; greater understanding; inner wisdom; compassion; kindness; love; joy; and of course, deep peace.

For when we tame our minds, when we release ourselves from its untrue stories and stressful dramas and misinterpretations and fretful disaster-planning, we can abide in our true nature.

Love.

And that is found deep in your heart.

And what I wish most for you is that you experience the deep wisdom, healing and peace found within your heart, and that its whispers become so precious to you that they enable you to tame your fretful mind and live from the loving guidance of your heart, and the peace that lies within.

With so much love,
Stella x
July 2018

Peace Lies Within

Get Out of Your Head

Where are you living? No, I don't mean which town, or whether you're in a house or apartment.

I mean, what space do you occupy? Do you live in your mind or do you inhabit your body?

It's a good question to ask yourself because in our busy lives it can be all too easy to occupy just the top two inches of our body and live in the mind.

And when we live in our minds, we're rarely present and never peaceful. We over-analyse the past and fret about the future. We're at the mercy of the to-do list in our heads. We lose perspective. We might fly off the handle at the merest provocation. Or we might get stuck in a permanent daydream, disappearing into our thoughts.

Occupying the mental plane of existence disconnects us from our body. Our breath becomes shallow, and our muscles get tense and tight. We ignore our body's needs too, or even stop noticing them at all.

When we ignore our body, such as its need for regular movement, rest and relaxation, and wholesome nutrition, we cut ourselves off from our physical foundations. Living in our heads, we lose a sense of stability, safety and security. And this can manifest as feelings of fear and anxiety.

So, in this section, I offer you practices and perspectives to enable you to feel more grounded; to get out of your head and into your body. To bring you out of the past, and back from the future, into the here and now.

I begin here because this is the foundation of taming your mind and reconnecting to inner peace.

If you're not grounded because you're lost in your thoughts, you are ALWAYS going to be at the mercy of your mind rampaging around like a bolting horse — pulling you this way and that and making you feel fearful, lost and out of control. Believe me, I know this from experience!

Let the guidance in this section of the book lead you back to a sense of safety and stillness, and give you some tools to recover your equilibrium whenever you're feeling off-balance or overwhelmed.

*

1. Be where you are

These words from the Buddha are a powerful reminder as to why it benefits us to live in the present: '*As you walk and eat and travel, be where you are. Otherwise you will miss most of your life*'.

So true. Yet such a challenge.

Living with mindful awareness of what we're doing, experiencing, thinking and feeling can bring such a sense of freedom.

And the Buddha gives us some practical tips here to help us along the way.

As you walk, just walk. Notice the action of your body. Notice your feet connecting with and lifting from the ground. Notice your surroundings.

Most of us (myself included) often don't notice how we got from A to B.

We've been wondering what we're going to do when we get to work. We've been worrying about our performance or the outcome of a business meeting. We're judging other people's appearances as we pass them. We're planning what we'll cook for the evening meal. We're musing over last night's episode of some soap or drama we've been watching. We're thinking about someone else and wishing our lives could be more like theirs.

When you eat, notice the taste of the food; the texture; its temperature; be thankful for its goodness (or if you're eating burger and chips perhaps be mindful that you're eating something with not a huge amount of goodness in it, and enjoy it anyway!). Put down that magazine; turn off the TV and be here now! Just eat, just drink. Slowly and with awareness. Your digestion will thank you for it.

When you travel, switch off the music, put down your smartphone and look about you. Notice the diversity of the people around you as you walk down the street. Notice your surroundings as you look out of the train window. Breathe and allow yourself some quiet time as you drive. If the bus is rammed, notice any feelings of frustration and discomfort that may arise. And breathe.

Our lives are ridiculously busy. Many of us rush around attending to all those plates we have spinning, worrying that one is suddenly going to crash to the ground. We're bombarded with noise and distraction. Our senses are in meltdown through overload.

We are at risk of rushing through our lives without noticing what's going on. It's like we're hurtling through our lives on a train at top speed with the blinds down. We're moving forward, there's an awful lot whizzing past us, but we have no idea what's going on. We didn't get off at any of the stops, and when we reach our final destination, we may have no idea how we got there. And perhaps we didn't even want to go there in the first place.

So how about slowing down and enjoying the journey? Notice the here and now. Be glad, feel blessed to be alive — no matter your circumstances. Notice those little, life-affirming, glimpses of beauty; a raindrop on a leaf; the smile on a child's face; tree branches silhouetted against a winter sky; the sparkle of sunlight on frost; the warm hug of a loved one.

All we have is the present moment. The past has gone; the future is a mystery. This moment is the gift we are given every second of our lives.

Make the most of it with love and laughter. Be alive now.

Mind Taming Peace Mantra:

I choose to be here, now.

2. Give yourself time to stand and stare

Do you remember when you were a child, and you'd spend what felt like hours lying on the grass and staring at the sky?

Watching the clouds form and change and pass? Watching, with fascination, the colours behind your closed eyelids as the sun shone on your face?

Ah, those innocent pleasures of childhood. And having the time to enjoy them without question or guilt.

How often do you allow yourself time simply to stand and stare now?

I'm guessing not so much? Between work demands; your family's demands; all the life admin that keeps stacking up every day. The daily rush and never-ending demands on your time and attention. Stand and stare? You must be joking!

If you do get a few moments to yourself, chances are you're so exhausted that you flop down on the sofa and you feel guilty that you're 'relaxing', so you push on through to tick off the next task that needs doing.

I know how it feels.

BUT, I also know, because I feel it myself, that there's a little part of your soul — a quiet but insistent voice within — that keeps tugging at your sleeve, as it were, saying 'look, isn't that flower beautiful?' or 'listen, can you hear the breeze rustling the leaves? Isn't it divine?'.

It yearns for you to let yourself sit and watch and listen and notice.

If like me, you're a sensitive soul, you secretly love to stop and notice the simple pleasures of life all around you. The delicate, blooming beauty of flowers. The reflection of trees on water. The clouds. The birdsong. The whisper of wind through leaves.

When I'm out and about in nature the words 'what is this life if, full of care, we have no time to stand and stare' (from the poem by *Leisure* by WH Davies) often arise in my mind.

And isn't that true?

Truly, what is this life if we can't stop awhile and notice? Contemplate our surroundings?

If we can't press pause, breathe, look outside ourselves and our anxious, contracting minds?

Expand your awareness and watch a bird in the garden — it's so fascinating as they hop and flit about their business without a care in the world — reminding us that we are sharing our environment with other living creatures.

Listening to the breeze in the trees quietens the incessant chatter of our monkey minds and encourages us to have a mind like the sky; open, expansive, infinite.

Pondering the stars in the night sky brings perspective on the smallness of our planet in the mystery of life. It reminds us we are just one in over seven billion human souls on this planet circulating a sun, which is just one of the billions of stars in the universe.

Stand and stare and drink it all in.

Mind Taming Peace Mantra:

I gift myself time just to stand and stare.

3. Slow down and tune in

Slow down and relax into the simple pleasures of life.

Revel in the natural beauty all around you. The sights and scents.

Breathe. Be still. Let it all in. Indulge your senses and simply be here, now, in this present moment.

Sit quietly. Take some deep breaths to settle. Close your eyes if you feel comfortable.

Bring your awareness into your body and notice the sensations of your feet on the floor ... the sensations of the chair beneath you ... the feel of the fabric against your skin.

Notice the coolness or warmness of your hands and feet ... the air against your skin.

You might like to pick up something that is near to you and feel the shape and contours of the object, and how it feels in your hand and against the skin.

Turn your awareness to any tastes in your mouth. Just notice your tongue. Your saliva. Run your tongue over the back of your teeth and the inside of your cheeks to help heighten your awareness.

Now turn your attention to any scents or odours in your environment — and notice any strong emotions or memory associations that may come up. Smells can evoke strong reactions.

Whatever arises, let it be and let it pass.

Now become aware of the sounds around you ... let them drift in and out of your awareness ... there's no need to name them even ... just let pure awareness take them in and let them go.

Finally, open your eyes gently and observe the things you can see ... don't stare or peer or scrutinise ... let your awareness softly rest on something in your field of vision and just take in the colour, shape, size, textures ....

Then let your awareness soften and broaden to gently take in what's in your peripheral vision.

Come to your senses to soothe your busy mind.

Mind Taming Peace Mantra:

I tune into my senses to slow down

and feel more peaceful.

4. Quieten the mind

How does it feel when your mind is racing? When the monkey mind jumps from one thing to the other? When you're ruminating over the past or catastrophizing about the future?

Chances are there isn't much space for exploration there, but rather, pressure and stress and a whirlwind of worry. But in a quieter mind, there is space. Space to explore.

Space to believe that the seemingly impossible can become possible, because '*To the quiet mind all things are possible*' ~ Meister Eckhart

What helps you to feel quieter in your mind? Maybe it's going for a walk, or a swim, or a run. Maybe it's stillness and sitting with a cuppa and watching the birds or the clouds in the sky. Or maybe it's spending time with loved ones.

Whatever calms your mind, do it!

Connect to a still, silent spaciousness where all is possible. When you do something that brings you into the moment, you feel a greater sense of mental space. The body relaxes; the breath expresses itself more freely. Then you may notice spaces between each breath — those little points of stillness.

And then you may joyously notice there is space between the thoughts. Space to notice what you're feeling. Space to choose how to act. A blissful space of inner peace and calm.

A quiet mind where all is possible. In this quiet-mind space you can begin to dream and wonder, and feel your way forward in your life with joy.

Mind Taming Peace Mantra:

I quieten my mind and open to limitless possibilities.

5. Be mindful

Living mindfully means living here and now, with love and compassion — and without judgement.

I'm sure you've heard all about it!

But how do you bring it into your life?

Well, the good news is that you don't have to sit for hours on end in the lotus position to be mindful (though you can do that if you want to!).

Here are a few practical ways you can bring a loving and compassionate, mindful attitude to yourself every day:

Be non-judgmental: notice when you're judging yourself, your experience or other people. Notice, let it be and let it go. Aim to feel like an impartial witness to the constant stream of thoughts and judging and reacting to inner and outer experiences. Let go of the categorising and judging. Release the labelling as to whether something is 'good' or 'bad', 'better' or 'worse'.

Practise patience: cultivate patience towards yourself and others. Begin with yourself. You're trying your best. Be patient and trust in yourself. And also realise that the vast majority of people are just trying to do their best. But we may have different needs and objectives and different ways of communicating them — which is where the conflict comes in. Be patient and breathe before you snap or judge. I know this can feel challenging but keep trying; it's called a practice for a reason!

Act like you don't know: 'beginner's mind' is a Buddhist concept. It's about having no expectations of what is happening in the moment, and opening up to whatever you're experiencing. Let go of the 'shoulds' and 'ought to's'. It's really quite liberating.

Let go of striving: stop putting pressure on yourself to relax and be calm. We live in a results-obsessed culture. Can you cultivate trust instead? Yes! Take the action steps you need, and then trust that all will come in time.

Accept: practise acceptance of things as they are in the moment (and not the drama and stories our active imagination layers on top). Resisting how things are in the here and now wastes energy and interferes with inner peace. If something needs changing resolve to take the positive action steps you need. But don't waste energy fretting and judging.

Mind Taming Peace Mantra:

I am open, patient, and accepting.

6. Scan your body

Here's a simple technique to get out of your head and into your body: a mindful body scan.

You can listen to a guided version in the resources which accompany this book.

Lie down or sit comfortably.

Take a few deep breaths and close your eyes. Let your awareness rest in your body.

How does your body feel? Try not to judge the sensations.

No doubt your mind will try to judge how you feel, but remember, you're trying to get back into your body and out of your head so every time a thought comes up, take a deep inhale and invite the thought to dissolve from your mind with the exhale.

Can you feel where you're holding tension in your body? Scan through your body. Common places for tension are the buttocks, hands, shoulders and jaw.

Beginning with your feet ... how do they feel? Can you feel any tension there? On a scale of 1-10, where one is completely relaxed and ten is held rigid, how do your feet feel?

Scan your awareness through each part of your body and apply the scale where one is completely soft, at ease and relaxed, and ten is held rigid.

Bring your awareness to your calves, shins, knees, thighs ... hips, pelvis and groin ... buttock muscles ... abdomen ... lower back ... spine and muscles around the spine ... upper back and chest ... shoulders ... arms ... hands ... neck ... and face.

Pay particular attention to any areas where you know you have a tendency to hold tension.

Also, notice any thoughts of 'I don't know how I feel' there.

When we live in our busy minds, we can feel cut off from our body, so the process of awareness is a practice too. Don't give up.

Wherever and whenever you feel tension, breathe out deeply and, with a gentle voice of loving kindness, tell yourself 'I don't need to hold onto this tension. I can let it go. I let it go.'

Place your hands over your heart and let out a long sigh.

Let your sigh be an exhalation that soothes.

Sigh the breath out, soften your heart. Let the emotional wounds heal. Let their burdens lift.

Mind Taming Peace Mantra:

My body reflects how I truly feel.

7. Accept how you're feeling

Where do you hold tension?

We all have a place where we feel it most.

It might be in your back; your jaw; your shoulders. It might be in clenched fists or tightness in the chest or throat, or perennially clenched buttocks!

Maybe holding tension has become so habitual that you don't even realise that you are tense.

For me, tension manifests in my shoulders, throat and often my jaw.

Our busy, fretful, planning, judging, rarely-present minds create this chronic tension in our bodies.

So, it's time to come out of your head and into your body. Listen to your body, and it will show you its wisdom.

And it's definitely worth listening, because often the whispers of tension will become shouts of pain or illness if we ignore them.

But, a word of caution.

Be kind!

We can so easily berate ourselves and mentally beat ourselves up because we're tired of feeling stiff and tense and having a mind that runs away from us at a million miles an hour.

But berating yourself just adds to the tension.

It doesn't make you feel any better, does it?

'You've been criticizing yourself for years and it hasn't worked. Try approving of yourself and see what happens.'

Wise words from Louise Hay.

So, try some kindness and self-acceptance instead.

Bring your awareness to your heart — the source of compassion within you.

Breathe …

Check in with your body … scan through your body from the crown of your head, through your face … neck … shoulders and arms. Your back … abdomen … pelvis and through your legs into your feet.

Whenever and wherever you feel tension in your body, gently remind yourself: 'I don't need to hold this tension in my body'.

Just whisper to yourself 'I can let this tension go.' Breathe. And allow it to be. Allow it to pass.

Bring awareness and gentle acceptance to whatever tension you're experiencing in your body here in this moment.

Notice the tension. And let it be. And gently suggest to yourself that perhaps you don't need it, and it's OK to let it go.

So, this might sound like a contradiction. Accept it AND remind yourself you don't need it?

Well, this first stage of accepting how you feel brings kindness into the equation; before the 'shoulds' and 'shouldn'ts' raise their ugly heads.

'My shoulders feel tense. They shouldn't feel like this. They should be relaxed. Why do I feel this way? I wish I didn't! …' is not conducive to relaxation!

Whereas 'My shoulders feel tense. This is just how they are. I breathe. I remind myself that I don't need to hold this tension in my shoulders ...' feels so much kinder, doesn't it? It gives you permission to relax rather than commanding that you must relax.

So, no pressure. No telling yourself you should be relaxed, or you should have everything under control.

Instead, hold your awareness within the space of your wise and compassionate heart.

Remind yourself that your natural state is relaxation.

But also remember that you can't create a relaxed state or force yourself to relax — you can only create the right conditions for the state of relaxation to arise.

You can do the same whenever your mind feels contracted or overwhelmed with thoughts. Gently remind yourself: 'I don't need to hold this tension in my mind'.

Be aware of how you feel.

Let your breath be free.

Remind yourself that you don't need this tension.

This tension is just a habit.

Maybe it had a purpose in the past. But now you don't need it.

And it is safe to let it go.

Mind Taming Peace Mantra:

My natural state is relaxation,

and so I gently invite the tension to release.

8. Notice your symptoms of relaxation

So often we focus on the negative sensations we experience in the body — signs of stress or anxiety, indications of a health condition or symptoms of something we don't understand.

It's perfectly natural to do this. It's our body's warning systems telling us we need to look after ourselves or get something checked out.

But how often do we focus on the sensations we feel when we feel good? Probably not very often!

So, try focusing on the symptoms of relaxation instead, this anchors positive experiences in your body within your mind.

Do you know what words you'd used to describe feeling relaxed? What feelings do you feel in the body?

For me it's feelings of a pleasant, grounded heaviness; a sense of spaciousness; my breath is free and deep and smooth. I feel alert and calm and that all is well.

How about you?

Take some deep breaths and stop creating tension. Let your naturally relaxed state take over.

How does it feel? Where do you feel it?

Can you let yourself feel the relaxation washing through you each time you exhale? Stop resisting. Let yourself relax. And recognise how it feels when you do relax. Remember it.

And know that this is your natural state.

Mind Taming Peace Mantra:

I let myself feel how good it is when I relax.

33

9. Walk here now

A simple walking meditation is a wonderful way to bring you out of your mind and into your body, creating a feeling of stability and security by connecting to the earth.

Do this outdoors if you can, in your garden (no matter how small!) or in your home if you don't have any outdoor space.

Stand still to begin. Feet hip-width apart; knees soft; draw in your lower abdominal muscles to support your lower back; let your spine lengthen; soften your shoulders; let the crown of your head lift subtly towards the sky.

Really feel your feet on the ground. Know that the solid earth is beneath you and that gravity will always keep you connected to that support.

Then slowly begin to walk, peeling one foot up on the in-breath and then placing it down heel first on the out-breath, and when the toes come down, then you begin to lift the heel of the other foot.

It feels beautifully nurturing to use these words as you walk — as taught by the Buddhist Monk Thich Nhat Hanh: breathing in 'I have arrived' breathing out 'I am home'.

Take maybe ten steps and then stand in stillness, before slowly turning around and retracing your steps. Breathe. Feel into each step. Be in the present moment. Let the thoughts subside. When the thoughts intrude, return to the feeling of walking: lifting the foot, moving the leg, placing the foot back down on the floor with intention.

Walk yourself home to inner peace.

Mind Taming Peace Mantra:

I walk in peace.

10. Connect to the earth

We spend so much time in our thoughts and on computers and mobile devices that we can get lost in abstractions and feel distracted and out of touch with our body.

Here are some simple tips to help you feel more grounded present and calm:

Walk on the earth: barefoot or in shoes, whichever floats your boat. Walk slowly feeling into each step as you lift then place each foot. Connect to the healing vibes of the earth.

Touch a tree: I like to hug an old tree whenever I see one. Touching a tree connects you immediately to something stable, something that isn't going to flit away like your mind! OK, this sounds a bit tree-hugging-new-age-crazy-hippy, but I promise you, it works! (Though do ask the tree's permission first.)

Eat: something like cheese, nuts or some dark chocolate. Nothing too sugary or full of caffeine. Something simple and solid to bring you back into your body. Eat it slowly and mindfully bringing your mind's attention onto the sensations of eating.

Sit or lie on the ground: sit, come down to all fours or lie-down. If you're up in your head, literally getting close to the ground helps to stabilise you and to feel the support of gravity keeping you safe on the earth.

Connect to strength, stability and inner peace.

Mind Taming Peace Mantra:

I am connected to the peaceful stillness of the earth.

11. Be like a tree

'A tree with strong roots laughs at storms' ~ Malay Proverb

How grounded are you? How easily do you feel knocked off balance by the ups and downs of life?

If your answers are along the lines of 'not very' or 'what does that mean?' and 'easily' then you need to develop your roots.

The pressures and demands of life can easily disconnect us from feeling secure and safe.

We get stuck in the stress response with our minds spinning like a tornado.

And if like me, you're sensitive to your surroundings and other people's moods, then you're going to be picking up on everyone else's energy and their ups and downs, which, added to your own can lead to storms of emotions up-rooting you on a daily basis.

So, how do you develop roots?

I find the most effective way is to get in touch with the body, specifically my legs and my feet. Get barefoot, march on the spot, bend and straighten your legs. Really FEEL the strong muscles in your legs and the contact through the soles of your feet with the strong, solid earth beneath you.

Try this antidote to anxiety to help you calm your body and mind: **Grounding Visualisation**.

> 1. Sit (on the floor or a chair) with your spine tall. Close your eyes or lower your gaze.

> 2. Breathe deeply and steadily and allow your breath to slow down naturally.

3. Take your awareness and your breath down to the base of your spine.

4. See in your mind's eye that a tap root is growing out from your tailbone down into the earth, holding you still and safe and steady on the ground. Nothing can pull or push on you now. You are held by the earth. You are supported. You are nourished.

5. Let any excess nervous, anxious energy drain away from you, down through that root. Allow this excess energy to seep away to be neutralised by the gentle, loving power of the earth, leaving you feeling still, safe and refreshed. Know that you can let go of physical tension and emotional turmoil down into the earth. Breathe deeply and let it all go.

When you're grounded and feel strong and focused and steady in your body and mind, then you can withstand the storms of life. Maybe even laugh at them — or just give them a wry smile.

Mind Taming Peace Mantra:

I choose to feel grounded, safe and secure.

12. Get it down on paper

Did you write a diary when you were younger? I did. Lots of us did in our youth. It was a way to find your voice; to express the frustrations of growing up; to test boundaries; to share your secrets with someone (even if it was just yourself).

I stopped this practice somewhere along the line — maybe you did too.

And then I came across something called 'Morning Pages' advocated by Julia Cameron in her book *The Artist's Way*.

When you get up in the morning, you literally write three pages in your notebook of whatever is in your head as a stream of consciousness. It doesn't have to make sense or be important. It's a process of clearing all the stuff that keeps rattling around your mind. You know, the, 'oh I must get that dripping tap fixed' or 'that messy drawer full of bills needs sorting' or 'I really should email my friend, I haven't been in touch with her for ages'; the daily stuff which mumbles away in the background of your mind, sucking up energy!

I did them religiously for a few months. And it did indeed release a huge creative surge in me — I started painting!

Now I journal as and when the mood takes me.

I work through something that I'm fretting about by writing down; whatever comes to mind about it. Or I reflect on my shifting mood as I cycle through the month and the seasons.

The point here is to get the thoughts out of your head.

By writing them down, you're releasing them from the cage of your mind where they tend to flap around like a caged bird; creating a lot of noise and disturbance. Writing seems to open the cage door. The thoughts will fly away!

Journaling helps to create clarity where there was confusion; it unsticks sticky thoughts.

Once you've expressed it in words (or drawing) on a page, you'll likely feel freer.

I highly recommend it. It creates headspace; it shows you where your mental energy is caught up; it helps you create change and take action.

You could do a page in the morning or a page when you get home in the evening or last thing before you go to bed.

Empty your mind of the thoughts flying around in your head. Give them to your journal. Release them into words.

You don't have to read over them afterwards. Just let your heart and soul guide you. Write it out. You could even burn the pages at some future point.

Just write the thoughts down, and get them out of your head!

Mind Taming Peace Mantra:

I write down my thoughts to clear my mind.

13. Have a tantrum

There's nothing quite like channelling your inner toddler and having a tantrum. Unexpected advice maybe?

Now, I'm not advising rolling around in the middle of your office or the supermarket aisle and crying uncontrollably like your mum wouldn't let you have a chocolate bar. (Though if you do that and someone takes a video, please do share it with me on Facebook!)

Nor am I advocating weeping and wailing, 'it's not fair' because your boss won't give you the day off.

No, I'm talking about taking yourself somewhere quiet where you can be on your own and have a bit of a hissy fit as a means of letting go of emotional tension from your body and mind.

It's a way to get out of your head and tap into your body's innate intelligence. It knows — even if you don't consciously realise it — when something is bothering you and where you hold it in your body.

Start off by walking on the spot. Lift your knees high and swing your arms.

Then call to mind anything that has annoyed you in recent days or weeks; somebody who pressed your buttons; something that really aggravated you (I bet you can think of a few things already eh?).

Then start to stomp around, and have some fun with it. Stick your tongue out, blow raspberries, stick your two fingers up at the world. Make some noise!

Even lie down and bang your feet and hands on the floor in true toddler melt-down style.

And do it like you mean it: with intention.

Do it on purpose. Release the tension from your body. Let out all the suppressed frustration and anger and irritation.

Let it up and let it out.

See it as emotional cleansing. We all experience times during daily life, rightly or wrongly, where we can't say what we feel. We swallow our words and bottle up our emotions. It sinks into our bones and muscles and joints. It becomes trapped, stagnant energy, which festers. And we become tired, oppressed, stressed and overwhelmed.

Yes, it would be great if you could talk through these issues with friends and family and/or the people concerned in a mature and level-headed manner. But, let's be honest, who really does that all the time? (Nope, me neither.)

It's human to feel these complicated feelings. So don't beat yourself up.

Have a tantrum instead.

It doesn't matter what it's about. You don't even need to have something specific in mind. Even if your own life is the picture of rosy perfection at the moment, there's enough stuff going on in the wider world to get us feeling down, depressed and frustrated.

So, make this part of your daily self-care routine. Have a bit of a stomp about; stick your tongue out and your fingers up at whatever might be bothering you.

Let it out and let it through, then dust yourself down and continue with the rest of your day.

Mind Taming Peace Mantra:

I allow myself to release trapped emotional stuff

through mindful tantrums.

14. Give yourself a round of applause

... well, kind of!

I'm talking about a simple way to understand the difference between thinking and experiencing the felt sense of being in your body.

It's a simple mindfulness technique, and an excellent reminder to get out of your head and into your body.

Begin by looking at your hands for a few moments; look at the shape, colour and texture of your hands and nails.

Notice any distinguishing features and items of jewellery.

Now close your eyes and notice what thoughts you have about your hands.

Next, clap your hands together a few times, then shake out the hands vigorously.

Now close your eyes and feel into the sensations of your hands. What can you feel? Perhaps tingling and buzzing? Stay with the raw physical sensations.

Finally, reflect on the difference between looking at and thinking about your hands, and actually feeling the sensations within your hands.

What do you notice between the two experiences?

If you're anything like me — and the people I've shared this exercise with over the years — chances are when looking at your hands and thinking about them, there could have been judgments as to the age of your skin; the state of your nails; noticing you have chipped nail varnish; perhaps noticing frayed cuticles and so on.

The mind gets involved to label and judge.

But when we bring our sense of inner awareness to the felt sense of the hands — after waking them up with clapping and shaking — perhaps the experience was different?

Instead of thinking about and judging your hands, you actually felt them, as they are here in this moment.

That's what getting out of your head feels like — you feel physical sensations that bring you into the moment and out of the analytical mind which is so very rarely present.

So, give yourself a round of applause; you've come into the here and now!

Mind Taming Peace Mantra:

I experience the felt sensations in my body

to come into the here and now.

15. Take a dance break

Strong or challenging emotions can make us contract in our body as well as our mind.

We move cautiously; we hold tight, and we guard ourselves.

Anger can feel like a burning in the stomach. You might feel it as a clenching in the jaw or fists.

Doubt can feel like you're small and helpless.

Anxiety could feel like an icy grip around the heart or a stone in your throat.

In this way, the mind affects your body.

So, let your body improve your mental and emotional state through movement.

Get up, move, stretch.

Put some music on and dance around the room like nobody is watching you.

Let the trapped emotions in your body move through and out. You don't even need to know what the specific emotions are or what they're about.

If you're feeling stuck on an emotional rollercoaster, breathe deeply and move freely.

Shift the energy.

Because when you move your body freely and let it move how it wants to, you really do shift something inside.

You'll change your mental state for the better. You'll breathe more deeply and bring more oxygen to your brain. You'll ease out tensions from your body.

Just let go. It doesn't matter what you look like or whether you're in time with the music. Have some fun!

Move with joy and let the joy that is deep within you bubble up to the surface.

Mind Taming Peace Mantra:

I move my body freely to shift stuck energy.

16. Have a laugh

Never underestimate the power of laughter, and that you can fake it 'til you make it!

Laughter can release pent-up stress and tension from your body and mind.

It's a great mood-booster. It helps us to relieve the feelings of difficult and strong emotions. It helps us shift our perspective.

Consciously smiling and laughing for no reason fools your brain. Part of it registers that you're smiling and signals the release of the feel-good chemicals serotonin and endorphins, which make us feel happy, (and can also reduce the perception of pain) and reduce the stress chemical cortisol in the body.

So, start off by saying, 'ha ha ha, hee hee hee'.

Smile and keep repeating, 'ha ha ha, hee hee hee'.

Stand up and move your shoulders up and down with it, 'ha ha ha, hee hee hee'.

Let your whole body move as you keep on going, 'ha ha ha, hee hee hee'.

Yes, it might seem strange and forced at first.

But keep going, 'ha ha ha, hee hee hee'.

Soon the laughter will spontaneously become genuine. You'll have no idea what you're laughing at, but it's something mightily hilarious because you just can't stop!

Try it.

How does it feel?

Laugh regularly, and soon you'll feel less stressed; less overwhelmed; more resilient; better able to cope with the challenges of life; and more peaceful.

Mind Taming Peace Mantra:

I laugh every day, whether I feel like it or not.

17. Shake it off

Have you ever noticed how animals shake sometimes? If you have a cat or a dog, you may have seen this. When they wake up, or after eating. Or after having a bit of a disagreement with another animal, or experiencing something stressful.

They give their bodies a good old shake out that kind of says 'Ok that's done, what next?'.

We can do the same!

Shaking your body releases tightness from the muscles and joints, and releases the feelings and effects of stress from body and mind.

It's like a reset button.

When you shake out your body and release muscle tension, this signals to the brain that you're safe (because if your body feels relaxed, the brain receives the message that you're not under attack, and so it's safe to relax further).

Shaking out your body resets the nervous system, because when you feel relaxed you're moving into parasympathetic nervous system dominance, which is the 'rest, digest and heal' response of the body, (as opposed to sympathetic nervous system dominance 'fight, flight or freeze', which can be our default setting in our pressured, busy lives).

Shaking your body is good for your circulation, and stimulates the lymphatic system, helping to drain away toxins, so it supports your immune system too.

And it's great for your emotional health too.

Shake off your worries, doubts, and fears.

So, give it a try.

Put on some upbeat music, stand up and shake out every single part of your body.

Shake your feet. Shake your legs. Shake your hands and arms.

Get those shoulders moving.

Shake your hips and your bum.

Shimmy. Move. Laugh. Let it go.

Shake it off!

(Top tip: Taylor Swift has the perfect piece of music to 'Shake It Off'!)

Mind Taming Peace Mantra:

I shake it off.

18. Retrain your brain with a mantra

What message is your chattering monkey mind giving you?

Do you have a little voice in your head giving you a running commentary on everything you do, say, think or feel? A negative mantra that you keep repeating?

I reckon that the answer is 'yes'.

Because we all do.

We all have a voice in our head running a commentary on ourselves, our lives and other people.

An inner critic judging what we do or say, replaying situations over and over again looking at what we 'should' have said or done. Analysing every waking moment and action we take, or fretting over what we think we should do, or ruminating over what might happen.

You're not alone in this.

Researchers have calculated that the average person thinks between 50 and 70,000 thoughts a day—that's between 35 and 48 thoughts per minute per person.

And that about 80% of these thoughts are negative.

They've also calculated that 98% of these are the same as the thoughts we had yesterday.

So, we can see a lot of these thoughts are down to habit: habitual thinking.

For whatever reason, at some point in your life, you began to tell yourself negative stories about yourself, and they've stuck. Often these are linked to events that happened in childhood.

Perhaps a teacher told you that you couldn't sing, leading to a limiting belief that you couldn't sing. A parent or carer said you're too quiet or too loud, so you spend your whole life telling yourself that you're shy or that you're too much.

You experienced something embarrassing in front of a classroom of your fellow pupils, and you live with the story that everyone is judging or laughing at you.

And when something triggers these memories in adult life, you go back to being the embarrassed or shamed child.

But these stories and reactions are just neural pathways in the brain that have become well-worn.

We humans are creatures of habit, and the brain will follow the path it's most familiar with.

There's a phrase in neuroscience: 'what fires together, wires together'.

What began as a reaction to someone or something appearing to attack you in subtle ways — such as questioning your ability or knowledge or judgement — can become an ingrained negative habit of self-talk.

I'll share with you an example from my life.

When I was at primary school, we were all made to try-out for the school choir. I didn't want to do this but had no choice. We had to sing 'Morning Has Broken' en masse with teachers coming around and standing at our shoulder and listening to us. If you weren't up to scratch, they tapped you on your shoulder to sit down, a gesture indicating you weren't good enough for the choir.

I didn't have a great amount of confidence in my ability to sing as it was, and as the teacher got nearer, my throat began to tighten. She eventually reached me just as the tune went really high. I can still remember the horribly strangulated sound that squeaked out of me — just before I received the 'tap of shame' on my shoulder.

That led to a LONG time of me telling myself I couldn't sing; it became an ingrained 'fact' in my brain. And if I had to sing when others could clearly hear me, my throat would tighten, and an 'interesting' noise would come out.

On my own though? A different matter. I LOVE singing! In front of an audience? No way.

We've all got these examples hidden in our past.

Experiences that led us to question our ability, so we shut ourselves down and kept telling ourselves we can't, or we shouldn't, or we won't. It all adds to the negative self-talk.

They're just habit patterns though, imprints left on the mind by experience. You can change these habits.

Instead of being at the mercy of your noisy mind, wouldn't it be great if you could consciously change the words your mind's inner voice uses?

The concept of neuroplasticity is a beautiful fact. Our brain adapts. When we do new things or think new thoughts, new neural pathways are created.

Each time we repeat an action or thought these neural pathways get stronger and more clearly defined.

It's as simple — and as challenging — as noticing your self-talk and becoming aware of the mood-music within your mind.

And then taking back some control and giving your mind a job to do, rather than letting it wander off on its usual record of worrying, fretting, ruminating, and judging.

A great way to take back this control is through the use of mantras.

Using mantras gives your mind a job to do.

A mantra is a chosen thought that you repeat and repeat and repeat, that's all it is.

Yes, there's a lot more to it than that if you choose to delve deeper, but at its simplest, a mantra offers us a tool to focus the mind.

A mantra can be a simple word such as, 'peace' or 'calm' or a phrase 'it is as it is' or 'today I choose to relax'. Or they can be 'I am' statements such as 'I am peaceful', 'I am calm', 'I am strong/courageous/resilient/loving' (or 'I have a beautiful singing voice') whatever qualities you wish to cultivate within yourself and focus on.

Or it might be a traditional yoga mantra in Sanskrit with sacred intention and vibration, such as, 'Om Namah Shivaya' or the Buddhist mantra, 'Om Mani Padme Hum'.

Repeating mantras — whether silently or out loud — helps us to calm the mind and balance our emotions; it evens the breath and quietens the thoughts.

It is soothing and soulful, calming and connecting.

Take back control of your mind and choose where you place your focus. So, what will your mantra be today?

Mind Taming Peace Mantra:

I give my mind a job to do with a mantra.

Peace Lies Within

Breathe Here Now

There are many circumstances in our lives that contribute to us feeling stressed, tense and overwhelmed. Some we can change (switch off our phone and stop checking our emails and Facebook before bedtime!). Others can feel a lot more challenging; the pressure of a job that doesn't fulfil you; the stress of our busy over-stimulating culture; the constant work of looking after children.

Perhaps all too often you find yourself in a place of overwhelm. That place where you can't think straight. You don't know where to begin. You're feeling irritable, frustrated, angry with yourself and the world. You have a tense jaw and shoulders and you're barely breathing. You can't focus.

Overwhelm gives you that feeling of barely keeping your head above water. Holding your breath. Headaches and sweaty palms from the stress. Feeling that you just can't cope. Wanting to run away from everything.

But in that moment, when overwhelm is getting the better of you, there is always something you CAN do.

Breathe!

It sounds almost too simple. It IS simple; powerfully so.

Stress and anxiety affect your breathing, it becomes shallow and tense as the muscles around your body — including those of the respiratory system — tense up ready to run or fight or freeze.

So, it makes sense that you can use the power you have to control your breathing to turn down the volume on your body's stress response.

When you breathe deeply, a strong signal is sent back to the brain, via the vagus nerve, that everything is safe and OK. This deep breath and message of safety will, in turn, trigger your parasympathetic nervous system response, enabling your body to relax and let go of some tension.

Conscious, steady breathing brings your nervous system back into balance, backing off from the stress response and enabling you to shine a light of perspective on what's going on.

The breath is the only physiological function controlled by both the involuntary AND voluntary branches of the nervous system.

The autonomic (involuntary) nervous system controls all of the processes that just happen without your having to tell them to, like the beating of your heart, digestion and breathing.

The somatic (voluntary) nervous system controls voluntary movement of the body via our skeletal muscles.

Breathing is also controlled by this voluntary system so that you can breathe intentionally. You can decide to lengthen and deepen your breaths to calm yourself.

Your breath is your friend. It accompanies you through life. You're always breathing.

With this section, I share simple, effective and powerful techniques and perspectives to help you harness the power of your breath, tame your mind and your body's stress response and feel more in control, settled and calm.

*

19. Let go of the battle

Life brings its challenges, it always will. But how much of our suffering around these challenges is caused by our own mind? By the internal battle we create as we resist what is happening or what we're feeling?

A BIG percentage I'd say.

How can you deal with your chattering mind? Sometimes it feels impossible to shut the pesky thing up!

If you feel you can't control your mind, then know you CAN control your breath, and that the two are intimately connected.

Take some deep breaths and notice the sensation of the cool in-breath at your nostrils and the warmer out-breath ... keep breathing ... keep noticing.

Breathe and let your eyes relax ... feel your face soften ... let your shoulders melt down away from your ears ... Just continue to breathe ... let the thoughts melt away ... sink into this moment.

Exhale ... let go of the battle.
Exhale ... let go of the busy, conflicting thoughts.
Exhale ... let go of the tensions in body and mind.
Exhale ... let things be.
Exhale ... come home to now.
For here in this moment ... all is well.

Are you feeling calmer now? Does your mind feel a little steadier? Yes? THAT'S the power of the breath! Breathe, soften, open. Let go of the battle and let this moment be.

Mind Taming Peace Mantra:

I breathe and let go of the battle.

20. Connect to your breath

When your head is full of thoughts; when you're worried or scared; when you're tired and just can't be bothered anymore; when you're tense; when you're in pain; when you're so overwhelmed that you think you're just going to go into melt-down; when burnout feels around the corner:

It can feel impossible to know what to do.

But there is something you can always do to help yourself. To reconnect back to yourself. To self-soothe. To come back from the brink.

I know because I've experienced all of these myself. The tension, overwhelm, exhaustion and whizzing mind.

They still sometimes creep up on me, but now I know what to do to stop them in their tracks and recover my equilibrium.

I take these simple steps: I breathe, and I reconnect to my body.

Try it.

Stop. Breathe. Notice what's around you. Notice what's within you.

Let in the joy of just being.

Breathe into this moment:

Let your awareness rest at the tip of your nose ... feel the air flowing in and out ... the cool in-breath ... the warmer out-breath.

Feel the sensation of the air as it flows into your body ... and up and out again.

Let the breath be natural and easy and flowing ... relax the belly ... soften the shoulders.

If your mind wanders, silently count the breath ... breathe in one ... breathe out one ... breathe in two ... breathe out two and so on.

And keep going for a few minutes at least.

Now, how do you feel?

Make friends with your breath. Tune into the constant ebb and flow that brings life to every cell of your being each and every moment of every day.

Breathing is an unconscious act. But when we bring our conscious awareness to it, we can tap into its awesome potential to change the way we feel for the better.

Whenever your mind feels scattered and distracted, or the sheer volume of your thoughts feel overwhelming, use your breath to refocus and quieten the mind.

Mind Taming Peace Mantra:

I connect to my breath to connect to calm

and peace and joy.

21. Stand upright and breathe

'An upright posture and a few relaxed breaths can make a great difference' ~ Buddha

A beautifully simple-but-so-true statement from the enlightened one (by the way, don't forget, we all have Buddha-nature inside us, so we're all enlightened really; it's just that life experiences, our mind and the culture of our society conspire to make us forget).

So, if you feel tired; if you feel anxious; if you feel stiff and achy; if you're scared of doing something; if you're so busy you don't know where to start; if you're in the middle of an argument — take a moment to lift your breastbone, open your heart and breathe deeply — you will feel better for it.

If you're feeling happy; if you're having a great time with friends or a loved one; if you're enjoying some lovely food; if you're watching a great film; if you're out for a walk on your tod — the same applies.

Lift and lengthen through your spine and the crown of your head. Sit or walk tall, breathe and you'll connect to the present moment and enhance your enjoyment even more. Focus on your posture, to allow your lungs to move, to open your heart space and to breathe well.

This simple shift in your posture will bring amazing changes to encourage your body to feel more aligned; your breath will flow more freely; you'll stop walking around looking at the ground lost in thought; and you'll feel more connected to the here and now: more engaged in life.

Lift and lengthen. Stand tall. Feel strong and open. Let the breath flow. And enjoy the difference this makes in how you feel.

Mind Taming Peace Mantra:

I stand tall. I breathe here, now.

22. Drop anchor with your breath

Rest in the safe harbour of your breath so you can drop anchor into the sea-of-now in challenging times.

Breathe with awareness to come back from the brink of overwhelm.

When we're in a place of stress, our breathing becomes shallow, tight and fast.

Harness your breath to calm body and mind.

Sit and close your eyes for a few moments. Breathe. Don't try to change anything. Let the breath come, let the breath go.

And softly check in with yourself. Where do you most easily and readily feel your breath moving in your body?

It may be the sensation of the cool in-breath and the warmer out-breath at your nostrils. Or the delicate flow of the air over your upper lip.

It may be the feeling of the air as it moves through your throat.

Or maybe it's in the natural rise and fall at your chest and/or abdomen.

Identify the safe harbour of where you feel your breath in your body and use it as an anchor to feel safe and present when the seas of life get choppy.

Mind Taming Peace Mantra:

I feel the breath in my body

to feel safe in this moment.

23. Take from your breath what you need

Let your breath give you what you need. Feel it as an infinite resource, supporting you and nourishing you and calling you home to yourself.

If you're feeling tired, heavy and lethargic, then breathe IN life and energy. Feel the air dancing around you, supporting you, helping you to feel light and free.

If you're feeling anxious, stressed or wired, breathe OUT to let go of tension, let it be and let it go. Feel your feet on the ground and let the earth hold you. Wriggle your toes. Wiggle your fingers.

Breathe in deeply to draw in life, energy, positivity, calm, courage; whatever you need.

Breathe out fully to release stress, tension, toxins; whatever you no longer need.

Pausing for breath will always help you to feel better; to help you make a better decision; to give you perspective; to calm the anger; to raise your energy levels.

And if you ever doubt yourself, stop and pause and breathe.

And know that you are doing the best you can, you ARE good enough, and you are safe and loved.

Breathe deeply.

Breathe and receive the support that is within, and all around you.

Mind Taming Peace Mantra:

I allow myself to receive

the energy I need from my breath.

24. Breathe back to balance

When you're feeling off-kilter remember that conscious, steady breathing brings your nervous system back into balance, backing off from the stress response and shining a light of perspective on what's going on.

Counted breathing is a simple tool you can use during the day to turn down the dial on the stress response and come back into balance.

Practise it daily for a few minutes so that it becomes a new, positive habit.

Sit upright, let your spine support your body. Breathe out and let your shoulders and jaw soften.

Begin to watch your breath ... the rise of the in-breath ... the fall of the out-breath ... then start to silently count your breath ... steadily count to four as you breathe in ... count to four as you breathe out.

Let the speed of counting settle into what feels right for you. There's no right or wrong here. But let the speed of counting be the same for the inhale and the exhale so that you're balancing the length of the in-breath and the out-breath.

Now I know that it might feel like breathing isn't going to sort out all your problems, but believe me, it's a start.

Try this little test.

Think about something that is causing you stress — just for a few moments — and notice the effect it's having on your breath and body.

Now, keep that thing in mind but bring in the counted breathing practice from above.

What do you notice? Is it possible to feel the same level of stress when you're breathing deeply? The chances are the answer is 'no'.

Maybe you feel a little calmer, spacious, settled. Does the focus on breathing bring a chink of light of perspective to the issue?

Keep it up. Do this practice when you're feeling fine (or maybe just not quite as stressed as usual!) and let it become a new habit.

Train your brain and your body to lean into the support of your breath to give you space.

Realise that you can help yourself: you are NOT powerless. Focus on what you can do in THIS moment to help.

Breathe.

Mind Taming Peace Mantra:

I breathe back to emotional balance.

25. Centre yourself

Feeling out of balance? Try this simple practice to tap into a sense of inner balance and equilibrium.

Adopt a relaxed yet alert standing or sitting position with your spine aligned and upright.

Focus on the way your spine lengthens and expands as you breathe in, and how it relaxes and softens in a subtle wavelike movement as you breathe out. Repeat this for a few rounds.

Now, as you breathe in imagine you are drawing light in through the crown of your head and down into your heart.

Breathe out from your heart, visualising the light flowing down through your body, your legs and feet and into the earth.

Breathe in and draw the light back up from the earth and into your heart.

Breathe out, taking the light up from your heart and out through your crown.

With each breath feel yourself filling with light and joy.

Connect to the strength of the earth beneath you and to the open, vast, limitless sky above.

Continue breathing in this rhythm for as long as you feel comfortable. Centre into your body with your breath.

Mind Taming Peace Mantra:

I am balanced. I am centred.

My body, mind and spirit are one.

26. Learn to let go

Human beings like to hold on.

We hold on to fears, disappointments, resentments, grief, anger and frustration.

Holding on to ideas of how things 'should' be.

Clinging to what feels good; fearful in case it disappears. Pushing away what we don't want.

All this holding on causes physical tension in our muscles, joints and tissues: we hold our issues in our tissues!

We build up an emotional armoury within our body.

And it doesn't feel good.

So, move, breathe, stretch, release to feel light, easy and joyful.

Let go of what no longer serves you.

Exhale ... release and let it go.

Make it intentional.

Breathe in and say to yourself a silent 'let'.
Breathe out silently say 'go'.

It's as simple as that. Repeat, repeat, and repeat again.

Do this as many times as you need until you feel the stress, anxiety or tension fading.

Say it like you mean it; LET ... GO .... If appropriate say it out loud!

Use your breath. Breathe in a sense of expansion, breathe out any tension. Breathe in relief, breathe out release.

Let ... Go ... invite your shoulders to relax.

Let ... Go ... feel your jaw unclench.

Let ... Go ... allow your breath to calm your body and mind.

You can take one minute or ten over this.

You can do it at your desk; stuck in your car on your commute; at home surrounded by candles and soft music; or in the middle of the night when you're mulling over pesky work problems and your mind won't switch off.

Let ... Go ... with each exhalation. Just as your breath is doing every moment of your life. In this way your breath can be your biggest teacher.

Breathe back into balance: let go of what doesn't serve you.

Mind Taming Peace Mantra:

I release what no longer serves me.

27. Settle your focus

Each and every moment we have so much going on, so much to pull our focus hither and thither.

All this jumping from one thing to another depletes our energy.

And it becomes a habit. Checking social media while you're reading a magazine; while eating your meal in front of the TV. Ever done that? (Yup, me too!)

In this over-stimulating world, we can all do with retraining ourselves to focus.

For when we focus on the thing or person in front of, us we can feel so much more grounded and present.

And it can be such a simple practice to bring into everyday life and helps us to cultivate feelings of calm, stillness and joy.

Take a few moments just to gaze at something.

Maybe a flower or a candle or a crystal or simply your thumb.

Settle, take a few moments to be still and just be with the object of your attention. Gaze at it.

Give it your FULL attention as you breathe deeply, steadily and smoothly.

Notice the colours ... notice the shapes ... notice the texture, size, shades of colour and contrast.

Be curious. Take it all in. Just gaze.

Let any thoughts come ... and go.

Breathe ... just watch ... be in the moment ... let nothing else matter for these moments.

Feel your body breathing and your mind settling.

How do you feel now? More present? Calmer? Still? Content?

Mind Taming Peace Mantra:

I give what is in front of me my full attention.

28. Take care of this moment

This moment is where we truly live. Yet our minds love to ruminate over the past and fret about the future.

So, keep coming back into this moment.

Feel your body sitting or standing or lying. Watch the breath. Tune into your senses.

Observe the thoughts but don't be pulled into them.

Look after this moment, and you will truly take care of your whole life.

It's as simple as focusing on your breath.

Breathe in ... and feel the sensations of the air flowing in through your nostrils and into your lungs.

Breathe out ... and feel the breath leaving your body with a sense of relaxation.

Give your mind something to do with this practice and silently repeat the words: 'I am breathing in ... and now I am breathing out'.

If you feel scared or overwhelmed or angry or doubtful, if you're experiencing any strong emotions, which are knocking you off balance, come back to your breath and keep repeating: 'I am breathing in ... and now I am breathing out'.

Repeat for as long as you like or until you feel a sense of inner strength, calm, contentment and a deep pool of peace within you.

Mind Taming Peace Mantra:

Now I am breathing in ... Now I am breathing out.

29. Show up

This moment is all you truly have in life.

The past is over; you can't change it.

The future is just that: in the future, yet to happen. Yes, you can influence what might happen in the future, but you can't control it.

The only place in which you can truly live, is in this moment.

Now!

Wake up to it.

Don't live a half-life of wishing you'd done something differently in the past or fretting about the future.

Wake up and live your life as it is unfolding. Now.

Show up.

Show up and be present with the person in front of you. Look into their eyes. Listen to what they're saying. Now.

Show up and be present with yourself. Feel your feelings. Allow them in and through. Notice when your attention wanders, breathe and bring your focus back to this moment. Now.

Show up and be present. Now.

I know it's not easy in a culture that is all about numbing out difficult feelings with TV, food, drink, social media or general busy-ness.

I know it's not easy with so much to distract your attention, and so many pressures and demands on your time.

I know it's not easy to feel what you're feeling, if what you're feeling is anger or sadness or frustration or anxiety or depression.

But it's more uncomfortable not to show up.

To feel your life slipping away in worry and fretting and not being in the moment.

So, show up to the glorious complexity of human life.
And live your life, here. Now.

Mind Taming Peace Mantra:

I choose to be here now.

30. Let it be

At times when your thoughts are overwhelming, or you're feeling sad or angry or frustrated or tired; choose this thought and make it your mantra:

'This moment is like this'.

This moment is how it is. Maybe you need to take action to change your situation at some point soon.

But this moment? Well, it's how it is. Breathe. Let it be.

So often we cause ourselves pain because we struggle with thinking we 'shouldn't' feel like this, or we 'shouldn't' be doing that.

And we berate ourselves for the struggle, creating layer upon layer of hurt.

Then we try to push the thoughts and feelings away and in doing so, cause ourselves more feelings of shame and frustration.

Try this instead:

Accept the feelings. Can you sit with them? What deeper messages do they have for you?

And let them be. Breathe. Let them go.

This moment is like this.

This anger is like this.

This sadness is like this.

This grief is like this.

This happiness is like this.

This joy is like this.

Let the thoughts and feelings come and go.

Unburden yourself of the pressure to have every moment filled with perfection.

Mind Taming Peace Mantra:

This moment is like this.

31. Comfort yourself with your breath

If you're feeling uncertain or off-kilter, practise feeling your breath. Tuning into the physical sensations of your breath brings you out of your thoughts and into your body.

This is a simple, comforting practice that you could do before bedtime to help you get a good night's sleep.

You can listen to a guided version in the resources which accompany this book.

> 1. Lie on your back with your knees bent and your feet on the floor, or on a sofa or bed.
>
> 2. Place one hand over your heart and one on your belly.
>
> 3. Move your hands until you find the spots that feel just right.
>
> 4. Pat gently on your tummy to draw attention to this area then pat gently or rub on the heart area to draw attention to this area.
>
> 5. Notice the surface you're lying on; feel where your back presses down into it.
>
> 6. Feel the sensations of your hands on your body.
>
> 7. Breathe in through your nose. Breathe out through pursed lips and feel the hand on your belly naturally relax down toward your spine.
>
> 8. Breathe in through your nose and let your belly rise and push your hand out, away from your spine. Breathe out through your nose and feel the belly and hand gently falling and moving in towards the spine.
>
> 9. Focus on slow, relaxed exhalations.

10. Continue breathing like this for a couple of minutes (or longer if you wish).

11. Finally, relax your hands onto your abdomen or on the floor by your sides, and now experience and feel your breathing in your whole body.

Let your breath be a source of comfort and safety.

Mind Taming Peace Mantra:

My breath brings me home.

32. Connect to the senses

Busy mind. Tired body. Feeling unfocused and sometimes overwhelmed. Sound familiar?

Our busy lifestyles and overstimulating environment mean that we're always on the go, and there's always something to do; there's precious little time to slow down and be.

There's a saying you may have heard: where your attention goes your energy flows.

If your attention is flitting around all over the place between past, present and future; getting lost in the past; fretting about the future; or judging and wanting to change what's going on now; then your energy is going to feel diffused and scattered: no wonder you're tired and feeling confused!

But you don't have to feel lost and out of control.

I'd like to remind you that we all have five things that are always available to us to bring us home; to drop anchor into the sea of now.

Your senses.

You can only ever truly experience your senses in the present moment.

You can't experience a beautiful sunset, which you saw a week ago (though you can remember it, which is a different experience). You can't smell or taste the meal you're going to eat tonight until that moment arrives of cooking and eating it.

Experiencing your senses only ever occurs NOW.

Remembering this is a powerful way to help yourself when you're feeling overwhelmed by events, thoughts or emotions.

A ship's anchor keeps it safely moored in the harbour no matter what gales blow, or how choppy the waters. In the same way, our senses provide an anchor to help us regain or retain equilibrium when the winds of change are blowing, or the choppy waters of intense emotions such as anger, grief, regret or fear churn us up.

It's really very simple, you just have to remember to do it!

So, make it a daily practice. Spend a few moments each day and focus on each of your senses in turn to come out of your head and into this moment.

Ask yourself:

What can I see? Just look around you and notice the colours, shapes and textures of what you can see in your immediate environment.

What can I hear? What sounds are coming and going? Just listen without judgment.

What can I smell? What scents are there? Food, perfume, plants. Just experience the scent without labelling or judging.

What can I taste? Is there any particular taste in your mouth at the moment? If there's no taste, notice that.

What can I physically feel/touch? Notice the temperature of the air on your skin, and where your body is in contact with the chair or ground. Feel into these physical sensations. Just stay with the raw physical sensation without judging or naming.

How does that feel? Do you feel more present?

Mind Taming Peace Mantra:

My senses bring me home.

33. Release anxiety

Try this when anxiety is rising within you.

As with all of these breathing techniques, it impacts directly on your nervous system, switching on your body's 'rest, digest and heal' response.

Sit upright, let your spine support your body. Breathe out and let your shoulders and jaw soften.

Begin to watch your breath ... the rise of the in-breath ... the fall of the out-breath.

And then start to silently count your breath ... count to four as you breathe in through your nose and count to six as you breathe out through slightly parted lips.

If/when that feels comfortable lengthen the out-breath to a count of eight.

You might like to bring in a mantra, a chosen thought, such as silently repeating 'I breathe in calm, I breathe out calm' or, 'I inhale peace, I exhale peace' (that's my favourite).

Let the speed of counting settle into what feels right for you — there's no right or wrong here — but let the speed of counting for the inhale and exhale be the same speed. And with that longer exhalation focus on letting go.

Letting go of the physical tension. Letting go of the thoughts crowding your mental space. Letting go of the pressure you put on yourself to be 'perfect' and have everything sorted.

Release anxiety and welcome in peace of mind.

Mind Taming Peace Mantra:

I release anxiety. I inhale peace; I exhale peace.

34. Tame tension

This simple visualisation is an excellent tension tamer. You can do it before you have to confront a stressful or challenging situation, or even in the moment itself!

Stand with your feet hip-width apart ... soften your knees ... allow your spine to gently lengthen up out of your pelvis ... relax your shoulders ... soften your face ... soften your gaze.

Breathe ... imagine roots bursting out through the soles of your feet anchoring you into stillness, safety and security.

Let any anxiety or nervous tension drain away ... let it be neutralised by the loving earth beneath your feet.

Anchor to the stillness within.

Calm the rage. Soothe the sadness.

Breathe and let a glimmer of a smile flicker across your face.

Dwell here in the present moment and be with whatever is present within you.

Allow ... receive ... and let go if you need to.

Breathe.

And allow a blissful calm to wash through you.

Mind Taming Peace Mantra:

I am safe. I am calm.

35. Tense and relax

With this exercise we consciously tense each part of the body then let it relax so we learn to feel the difference between the two sensations.

Sit or lie comfortably. Close your eyes if that feels OK for you.

Now go through the process of scanning through your body from your feet, slowly up to the crown of your head.

As you inhale tighten and tense the muscles in each area, exhale let go. Exaggerate the tension. Feel your breath holding too. Feel the stuck energy and tension. And exhale to deeply release and let go.

Begin by tensing your feet ... then calves and shins ... knees ... thighs ... hips ... pelvis ... groin ... buttocks ... abdomen ... lower back ... muscles around the spine ... upper back and chest ... shoulders ... arms ... hands ... neck ... face.

How was that? Stay for a few moments and just breathe here now.

Did you notice how you create the tension, and how the relaxation happens naturally when you consciously release the tension?

That's a really important lesson to learn.

Relaxation is a natural response that occurs when you create the right conditions. You can't force it!

When you come into the here and now and inhabit your body; when you breathe deeply; when you focus on a releasing exhale, relaxation will happen.

Relaxation will naturally happen when you stop creating tension.

And remember this Chinese Proverb:

Tension is who you think you should be. Relaxation is who you are.

Mind Taming Peace Mantra:

Tension takes effort. Relaxation is my natural state.

Make Friends with Your Emotions

Emotions. We all have them. It's an essential part of what makes us human: the capacity to feel.

Some we call good and embrace, others we call bad and try to push away.

All too often — perhaps uncomfortably so — we feel at the mercy of our emotions; like we're on a roller coaster that lifts us to the heights of joy, gratitude, trust, self-acceptance, abundance, confidence, clarity, love, connection, inspiration or serenity. Then all too quickly sends us plummeting into fear, worry, anxiety, doubt, grief, shame, anger, distrust, loneliness, confusion, stress, loneliness, or feeling broken.

This can be caused by hormonal fluctuations, external challenges, the thoughts we're thinking, and habit patterns of how we react to and approach life.

But all this being pulled this way and that by our emotions can feel incredibly confusing and even quite scary. It's as if we're riding an uncontrollable horse, which sometimes may be placid and other times running away at break-neck speed, and we have no control over its behaviour!

Sound familiar?

Do you wish you could train the horse so it would do what you wanted it to?

Now, as I say, experiencing emotions is a vital and beautiful part of our humanity, so I'm sure you still want to experience emotions. Numbing your feelings so you're always on a steady even-keel of not-feeling-much-at-all-ness is not something that would enrich your life.

But you're not alone if you wished you could have some control over the emotional ups and downs.

It can be incredibly helpful (and mind-opening) to understand the physiology of emotions; what's actually going on in your body when you're experiencing strong emotions.

This understanding can help lessen the feeling of being possessed by some kind of panicked gremlin which makes you your own worst enemy. It also provides perspective and enables us to realise that our emotions are not our enemies; they're messengers.

In this section, I share perspectives and practices to empower you to change your relationship with your emotional landscape. To make friends with your emotions so you can feel more grounded, aware and balanced and, of course, more peaceful.

*

36. Understand your emotions

Have you ever stopped to wonder what emotions actually are?

The word 'emotion' comes from the Latin *e-movere,* which means 'to move out'. So emotions can be seen as energy in motion. Something that is moving through you, and, in fact, needs to move through you.

So, what creates this energy that needs to move and be expressed?

It's a five-step process:

> 1. We experience stimuli, such as something happening to us; an interaction with another person; seeing something, for example, on the news or as we're out and about in everyday life. We also experience internal stimuli such as a memory or thought.

> 2. The brain responds. It compares these experiences with its library of memories — what we've experienced in the past — and labels it as safe or unsafe, good or bad, a comfort or a threat.

> 3. Chemicals are then produced within the body; stress hormones if the brain perceives a threat, or feel-good chemicals if the experience is positive.

> 4. The body responds to the stimuli and the production of these chemical messengers by, for example, creating muscle tension or butterflies in the stomach; or allowing the muscles to relax or a smile might appear on your face.

> 5.This response gives rise to feelings within the body and mind, which we label as emotions.

So, you can see that many of our emotional reactions are down to what we've already experienced in our lives. The brain has been programmed to respond by how we've reacted before.

And how we've reacted before most often began in childhood, and the messages and reinforcement of behaviour our parents/carers gave us.

These chemical reactions exist to ensure our survival. It's a good thing to feel some level of fear when you're crossing a busy road, for example. Otherwise, you'd stride out with complete abandon and be oblivious to the double-decker bus about to mow you down!

From our brain's point of view, anything that represents a threat to us will create a strong reaction, which we regard as difficult or painful.

But the threats the brain perceives are not always about buses about to mow us down. Anything that constitutes a threat to our sense of 'me' will be interpreted by the brain as a threat.

Anything that might compromise our sense of self; our emotional boundaries; physical space; sense of identity, will be deemed a threat and produce these strong responses to make us do something to protect ourselves.

So, a perceived insult feels like a threat because it is an attack on our sense of self and our identity. The brain interprets this as a threat to our existence and switches on the body's stress response: the fight/flight/freeze response. This response leads to tension and a pounding heartbeat that may flip into anger or trigger feelings of low self-esteem (or a toxic combination of both).

And the more we experience this, the stronger the reactions become; because we're training and programming our brain to respond to insults with stress and thoughts that question our self-esteem.

However, these chemical reactions are designed to provide us with enough energy to deal with the threat. Nervous system-wise we're still using an ancient operating system that evolved thousands of years ago to deal with the real threats of wild animals or attacks by other tribes. The stress response back then would literally be lifesaving.

Trouble is, the threats around us today are directed more toward our sense of self than to us physically. But our brain and nervous system have not evolved to know the difference. And they respond the same way and with the same intensity whether the threat is towards the sense of self, or towards the physical body. So a negative comment or insult will evoke the same response as would a lion on the attack. Fight or flee or play dead!

And while fighting or running away helps to discharge the stress chemicals running through our bodily systems, in modern life we usually have to put-up-and-shut-up, so those chemicals linger in the body, lodging themselves in our cells, in our spines, joints, muscles and internal organs. Building up an inner landscape of emotional toxicity, and training our brains to expect more of the same each time we're triggered.

Ah humans ... we're a complicated lot, aren't we?

Now, maybe you think that because your emotional reactions have been learned and reinforced every day of your life, that you're stuck on your own roller coaster and its vertiginous ups and downs.

You've always been a person who worries, or gets frustrated or angry. You feel like you've always had low self-esteem, so you're stuck that way.

Well, I'm delighted to let you know that while your 'frenemy' the brain is a sucker for reacting as it's always done, it also has an amazing capacity to change: to be re-programmed. It's mightily adaptable.

While you may habitually fret and worry and doubt and get angry, you can in fact, rewire your brain to react and feel differently.

Each time you learn something new, or as you become aware of your habits and begin to choose a different reaction to a stimulus, you're creating new neural pathways.

Each time you decide to let go of the feelings of anger or resentment or confusion and consciously focus on feelings of acceptance, gratitude or joy you're building new pathways in the brain.

And each time you reinforce these new pathways of acceptance or high self-esteem or kindness or love, they become stronger, and the old pathways fall into disuse.

How do we do this? Well, practices that help us to slow down and bring the nervous system back into balance are a good place to start. Going for walks and taking in our surroundings; relaxing activities you enjoy; mindfulness; yoga; relaxation and meditation. They all help us to slow down, breathe, relax and come out of the stress response and into a greater feeling of equilibrium.

As we relax, we become more reflective and less reactive. We start to see our emotional reactions for what they are: reactions based on habit. We can reflect on how we'd rather feel and consciously choose to release the anger and choose peace instead.

So, next time you're on that runaway rollercoaster, remember that actually, YOU are in charge. You can tame your mind and choose how you feel instead.

Mind Taming Peace Mantra:

I understand where my emotions come from.

I can choose how I wish to feel.

37. Allow yourself to feel

It's OK to feel angry.

It's OK to feel fearful or confused or full of doubt.

It's OK to feel irritated and frustrated.

It's OK to feel joyful or deeply content.

It's OK to feel happy or cheerful.

It's OK to feel baffled or bewildered or bemused.

It's OK to feel the depths of despair and the dizzy heights of bliss.

It's all OK.

It's OK to FEEL.

Experiencing emotions is part of being human.

That flow of feeling, sensation and energy is natural.

The trouble comes when you tell yourself that what you're feeling is wrong. Whether it's because it doesn't fit in with those close to you, or because it doesn't match what society says you should feel, or it doesn't fit in with your sense of self-identity (for example, 'spiritual people shouldn't be angry' or 'men should be strong all the time' or 'women are too emotional').

The trouble comes when you push the feelings down and bottle them up. They WILL make themselves known whether through dis-ease or explosive emotional outbursts — either way, it makes a mess!

The trouble comes if you become so attached to feeling a certain way — guilty or angry for example — that it limits your life and blocks your joy.

Or you become so attached to feeling light and blissful and joyful that you deny you feel anything challenging and the 'bad' stuff gets denied and pushed away.

But there's no trouble in having the feelings in the first place.

Denying, ignoring, numbing or grasping after emotions are what causes problems (plus it all takes so much energy!).

Try this instead:

Let the feelings in, sit with them a while.

Be honest. Be open. Breathe with the feelings.

Be brave and courageous and resilient; yes you can!

Ask the difficult emotions, which keep coming up, what message they have for you. Do you need to change something in your life? Do you need to learn to accept something you can't change?

But please remember. There's no need to be afraid of feeling.

Let the emotions in. Let them through. There's no need to judge.

Use their energy to inspire you to action and creativity and passion and change or acceptance.

It's OK to feel, my love.

Mind Taming Peace Mantra:

It's OK to feel emotions.

38. Take one day at a time

Working with our emotions, to understand where they come from, learning our habits of reaction, and choosing where to focus our energies is hard work!

It's rewarding and uplifting and soul-nourishing, but it can also sometimes feel like you're going around in circles as the same feelings and reactions keep on coming up again and again, slapping you around the face.

You might think you've come to understand why you fret about money so much. You've looked at the messages your parents gave you about lack and never relaxing in case money runs out. You've worked on your abundance mindset and learned to trust and go with the flow.

Then something happens — maybe it's talk of interest rates rising — and you're back in the, 'what if' scenarios fretting you won't be able to pay the mortgage. And the old fear of not having enough money rises up YET again.

Or perhaps it's feelings of low self-esteem. You've come to understand this is a pattern. Your brain's been trained this way by caregivers, schooling and a culture that trades on shame and provoking feelings of not being good enough.

Then you go on Facebook and see the friend request sent to someone you recently met still hasn't been accepted and you fret that they don't like you, or aren't interested in you. And the old 'not good enough' and 'I'm not interesting enough' feelings come flooding back.

It can be easy just to give up and give in.

To believe the lie that you can't change and never will, and there's just no point in trying.

When this happens, try telling yourself this:

'Just for today ... I will be peaceful.'

'Just for today … I will let my mind be at rest.'

'Just for today … I will be grateful'.

Focus on today. What can you do today to feel more confident or abundant or calm?

It doesn't matter how you felt yesterday; tomorrow will take care of itself all in good time.

What can you do today to understand why you're feeling how you're feeling?

What can you do today to find peace with your emotions?

This is a great lesson I've learned from my Jikiden Reiki practice.

In Reiki, there are Five Precepts that offer a way to live with greater equanimity, guiding us along the path to inner peace:

'Just for today; do not be angry, do not worry, be grateful, do your duties fully, and be kind to others.'

It's applied mindfulness: being in the moment and taking each moment as it comes.

Take one day at a time and resolve to live how you wish to live — just for today.

It takes the pressure off feeling the need to make grand, permanent and sweeping changes. To transform yourself. To put the past behind you once and for all. These are heavy burdens to put on your shoulders!

When you're feeling stressed or overwhelmed and anxious; when your mind is running away at a million miles an hour; it can feel calming and freeing to resolve that 'just for today' I will focus on feeling calm; happy; safe.

These precepts help us understand that all things change — our mental states and emotions too. It's how life is.

Yes, continue to work on yourself and to grow in emotional and spiritual maturity.

But also acknowledge with kindness and self-compassion that you do this with the choices you make and actions you take day by day.

Mind Taming Peace Mantra:

Just for today I choose how I feel.

39. Embrace it all

There's so much pressure to be always 'on', always doing, always hustling in case we miss out.

Miss out on what?

If we're honest with ourselves this constant busy, busy, busy is a way of numbing ourselves.

Our culture wants us numb, so that we consume in a frantic attempt to fix the pain we feel inside.

We may prefer to feel numb, so that we don't feel the painful emotions inside us.

But the pain is there because we're not stopping, slowing down and inviting a gentle, joyful gratitude for the good in our lives.

And if you're numbing what you don't want to feel, chances are you're deadening all of your emotions, including those feelings of contentment, joy and love, which uplift and inspire you to embrace life.

So, slow down. Breathe. Let yourself feel. Whether joy or pain or one of the million other feelings that may be present.

Feel them. Let them be.

Then choose to focus on the good in your life.

Be a radical. Be content.

Live awake.

Mind Taming Peace Mantra:

I bravely choose to feel all that I'm feeling.

40. Celebrate quiet courage

Modern life is challenging. Truth!

There are so many demands on our time and attention that sometimes even getting up out of bed in the morning can seem like hard work.

When you feel like it's all too much, breathe. Take a few moments.

Keep going.

Ditch the old saying of 'one step forwards two steps back' and replace it with 'two steps forward one step back'.

Celebrate the quiet courage of keeping on trying.

Our culture glorifies bigger, louder, better. Let's glorify small wins instead.

Quietly appreciate your inner strength if life is going to crap all around you.

It's courageous to let in your feelings and actually feel them while so many people around us are numbing themselves with social media, food, alcohol, busyness ....

If you embark on the path of self-understanding and development, you are swimming against the tide.

Most people — and I say this with zero judgment — are simply trying to get through life. Head down. Keep going. Don't rock the boat. Don't allow yourself to feel too much because it's uncomfortable.

But more and more people — and I think you're one of them as you're reading this book — are waking up and courageously lifting their heads up and saying, 'hang on, something doesn't feel right here. Is there another way?'. And it's courageous to do so.

The origins of the word courage come from 'cor' the Latin word for heart. This suggests to me a sense of our heart being our source of courage and bravery. It's our heart that enables and encourages us to embrace life and its challenges.

So when you feel the call to swim against the tide of your culture, it's your heart calling to you.

And it means change.

It means letting in the feelings. It means looking at your thoughts.

What you see and feel may well be challenging! But please don't give up when things start to feel difficult. Please don't put your head back down and live a half-life of numbed-out fogginess.

Let the tears flow. Beat up a pillow if you need to. Curl into a ball and wish the world would just go away.

And know, you will try again tomorrow.

Keep going, you'll get there.

Mind Taming Peace Mantra:

No matter what happens today,

I will try again tomorrow.

41. Let them come, let them go

So much of our tension, angst, stress and anxiety is caused by our mind and the thoughts and feelings that we can all too easily hang on to.

Feelings and emotions affect our body. The nervous system may be revved up or depressed. Our muscles tense.

Our posture changes, and our inner chemistry changes as stress hormones flood the body.

But if we can remember that these thoughts and feelings aren't permanent, we can begin to find an inner freedom and release.

Feeling angry? View it as a visitor within your being. Notice it. Let it come. Let it go.

Feeling sad? Same thing. Let it come and let it go.

Feeling frustrated? Don't attach to it or allow your mind to create added dramas about how you should and shouldn't feel.

Learn to watch your inner landscape as it shifts throughout each and every day.

And move your body — walk, stretch, dance and see if that shifts anything.

You'll soon learn which of these visitors go when invited, and which don't get the hint! You'll get to know yourself much better. And you'll learn which emotions are sticky, and which need some work to release. And release can be achieved through bodywork such as yoga, counselling or therapy, or emotional/energy healing such as Emotional Freedom Technique.

Treat all these visitors to the guest house of your mind/body with kindness and compassion and see what messages they have for you.

But never forget that they are just visitors — they are not permanent inhabitants.

They will come. And they will go.

Mind Taming Peace Mantra:

I choose to let the thoughts and feelings come,

I choose to let them be; I choose to let them go.

42. Learn to respond

Maintaining emotional balance. Aah, the holy grail!

Relief from the rollercoaster ride of our emotions that pull this way and that on a daily basis.

If we can learn to step back from the stories our mind weaves, and the dramas our mind and habits create, we can stop letting life and other people push our buttons.

We can create a space between stimulus and response. We remember to breathe; to take a moment. And to CHOOSE how to respond.

By connecting to how you feel physically, emotionally and mentally, you can retrain your brain to learn to reflect, notice and respond rather than blindly react and judge.

Did you know you can rewire your brain? When you experience new things or change your thoughts, you're creating new neural pathways. And ... what fires together wires together.

So, if you find you're about to lash out, judge or criticise yourself or someone else: stop. Take a breath. And ask yourself, 'Is this how I truly want to respond or am I reacting?'.

Keep practising this awareness during your daily life. Create a new positive habit of responding mindfully, with kindness and compassion, rather than reacting from frustration, fear or anger.

And this will help you to become less reactive and more reflective and accepting.

Mind Taming Peace Mantra:

I choose how I respond to life.

43. Choose joy

Joy, such an uplifting feeling. But one we might resist.

We might feel scared of embracing joy in case something bad happens to take it away.

We might resist joy because of the challenges we have in our life.

If this resonates with you, then I'd like to share something with you that will perhaps help to shift your perspective.

Over the years I have met people living with pain, disability, even terminal cancer who have been full of joy and life because that's how they've chosen to live the life that they have, even with the challenges they've been given

They decided to embrace the life they have.

They placed their attention on joy.

And it is a truism: energy flows where your attention goes.

It's all about how you approach life — because the energy you bring to life will hugely affect how you experience your life.

If your mind and your life were a garden, which would you choose to water? The flowers or the weeds? Because whichever you water will grow and flourish.

If you place your attention on what's wrong in your life, what you think you lack; and if you dwell on negative thoughts; then you will experience life as a struggle.

Place your attention on what you are grateful for and focus on life-enhancing and supportive thoughts in your mind. Then your experience of life will be more peaceful, positive and joy-filled — no matter the challenges.

I'm not talking about wandering around with rose-tinted specs and ignoring the challenging circumstances or difficult emotions that come with being human.

No, I'm talking about being with and dealing with the messy stuff that comes up through your life, and choosing to feel alive and vibrant anyway.

So, join with me and imagine life and light streaming through you into every cell of your being and affirm out loud — and really mean it: *I am filled with abundant joy and energy!*

Mind Taming Peace Mantra:

I am filled with abundant joy and energy.

44. Choose peace

'Before me peaceful, behind me peaceful, under me peaceful, over me peaceful, all around me peaceful ~ Traditional Navajo Prayer

Beautiful blessings to remember whenever you're feeling distracted, fearful, overwhelmed, tired, angry or anxious.

These challenging feelings can all too easily overwhelm us, and we get stuck in a place of mental tension and powerlessness.

To shift your energy, imagine yourself in a bubble of peace. You might see the bubble as light or feel it as a loving warmth.

What colour is it? How close or far away from you is it? There's no correct answer. Feel into it. Sense into the details. Make it feel real.

Feel how this cocoon of peace surrounds you, enfolds you and protects you.

Let in this feeling of deep peace, let it fill your heart and every cell of your being, and feel it supporting you through everyday life.

This is the peace within your heart radiating out to encircle and support you.

Feel it, know it and remember it is always there to protect and guide you.

Mind Taming Peace Mantra:

Peace flows towards me; peace surrounds me;

peace flows through me.

45. Choose gratitude

Consciously choosing to feel grateful is a powerful practice.

Now, I know that life can be challenging and that your health might not be what you'd like it to be. Perhaps family or colleagues are causing you grief. Maybe you're experiencing low self-esteem and find it difficult to be grateful for yourself, or you're worried about what's going on in the world and what the future holds.

Practising gratitude isn't about denying the challenges and difficulties you may be experiencing.

It's about choosing to feel grateful for the good you DO have in your life.

It's easy to get stuck in what we think we lack, or to become overwhelmed by the injustices in this world. In that headspace, you're likely to feel heavy and low in energy and defeated.

I don't believe you were born to live life in this way. You were born into a human body with a mind and senses and consciousness to embrace life.

Embracing gratitude and thankfulness for what you do have in your life lifts the spirit and raises your vibration.

If you can find any authentic reason to give thanks and place your attention there, well, science and statistics say that you're going to feel better on many levels.

There's a growing body of scientific research, which shows that people who consciously choose to live with gratitude, experience measurable physical and psycho-social benefits.

They experience more positive emotions and less depression; they sleep better; exercise more and generally look after their health. They express more compassion and kindness and feel greater empathy for others and enjoy higher self-esteem and stronger immune systems.

If you're stuck in a rut of challenging emotions such as doubt and fear and anger you're going to have more stress hormones flooding your system which, as I outlined in the introduction to this book, has long-term health impacts.

If you choose to lift yourself out of that rut and offer thankfulness, and if you reflect on even the little things you're grateful for, then you will shift your inner landscape and biochemistry.

So, take a moment. Take some deep, cleansing breaths.

And call to your heart, one person, thing or place in your life for which you feel grateful today.

Let that feeling fill your heart with gratitude. Sit and breathe with it for a few minutes.

Let your gratitude flow through you and out from you to kiss the whole universe.

Mind Taming Peace Mantra:

I choose to feel grateful for all that I am

and all that I have.

46. Melt the emotional ice

I usually recommend sitting with your emotions; inviting them in and making friends with them and reflecting on the messages they have for you.

But sometimes, you need to invite those emotions, stressful feelings and repetitive thoughts to go. To leave. To evaporate. To melt away.

Perhaps they've lingered too long. You've enquired within but still you feel stuck.

Or maybe you've just had a bad day and want to leave it behind.

Or perhaps your mind is busy, and you're not sure why you're feeling so weighed down.

For any of these situations or others like them, I recommend the following technique that has brought me, and many of my students, much solace when we needed to let go.

You can listen to a guided version in the resources which accompany this book.

> 1. Sit or lie down comfortably and settle into a nice sense of stillness ... let the breath deepen and slow down.
>
> 2. Allow the events of the last few days and any particular thoughts and feelings that are bugging you, to run slowly across your mind.
>
> 3. Visualise that the emotions you experience with each event start to evaporate like a blue mist that slowly starts to build up around you, getting denser and denser.

4. Just breathe and invite these emotions to evaporate and join the blue mist, which is growing denser and denser, surrounding you.

5. When you have released all of it, allow the blue mist to freeze and to become ice. Notice the beauty of these frozen emotions; now they are unable to hurt you.

6. Bring your awareness to the heart and begin to visualise a strong light burning there; like a candle. Let this flame grow hotter and hotter.

7. As it does so, you notice that the ice starts to melt. Water runs down it, and then a hole appears in the ice as the warm power of the heart melts through.

8. Continue to melt the emotional ice, allowing all of the negative emotional energy to flow away like water, unable to harm you. When all of the ice has gone, notice how calm and clear you feel. Have a sense of gratitude for feeling this way.

9. Let the light at your heart surround your whole body now ... filling your body, heart and mind with a deep inner sense of joy.

Then continue with the rest of your day feeling lighter and freer.

Mind Taming Peace Mantra:

I let challenging, lingering emotions melt away,

and I now feel light and free.

47. Let life flow

All of life is change. It's a truism that change is the only constant in life.

Nothing lasts, everything changes. Fashions change. Technology changes. The cells in our body continually die and replace themselves. Our breath comes and goes. Emotions and thoughts arise and fade. And, whether we like it or not, we are getting older: changing year by year. The seasons come and go.

Nothing remains the same.

Yet, how often do we want to hold onto the 'good' stuff and push away the 'bad'? We create inner conflict because we don't allow life to unfold, change and ebb and flow as it inevitably must.

Step back, endeavour to watch whatever happens in life with a sense of curiosity. Try letting whatever is, simply be. And perhaps you'll experience a greater sense of perspective and freedom.

Simply allowing can help you bring perspective when you're in the grip of strong emotions.

Fear and hurt will subside. Joy will return. And that will ebb and flow too.

It all changes. Let it flow. Let it be. It is as it is.

Breathe. Smile. And let life flow like a river.

Be kind to yourself. You're OK. In fact, you're more than OK! And here in this moment, all is well.

Mind Taming Peace Mantra:

I choose to relax and let life flow with ease.

48. Surf the waves of life

Life will always bring its challenges. Whether it's work, family, money, health, or our own monkey mind.

The waves are going to keep coming. Accept that. Let that be.

And learn to surf!

Surfers don't battle against the wave or try to control it or beat it. They don't try to fight it off. They roll with it.

But as humans we try to direct the waves of life; we resist and judge and try to control the reality of what we're experiencing.

It's a waste of energy and rarely makes a positive difference! Can you remember the last time resisting the truth of what was happening led to a positive change?

No, me neither.

It probably led to feelings of frustration, anger and doubt.

By surfing the waves of life, you accept what you're experiencing. You bring your awareness to what is happening now and to the truth of the situation (rather than the dramatic stories your mind will be making up) so you can move forward with intention and grace rather than flapping around in a panic or tantrum or sulk.

Pain and fear and challenges are part of what it is to be human.

They're the monster waves that can drown us if we ignore them.

We may spend our lives in fear of the waves that might be on their way.

But realise that you already have successfully surfed the waves at some point in your life.

Think of a challenging experience from your past. How did you get through it? Even if it feels a mess and you believe you could have handled it better, recognise that as you're here, reading this, you DID come through it. Reflect on the lessons you have learned from that experience.

Congratulations! You are a surfer of life's waves already!

So instead of worrying about the waves, centre and ground yourself. Regularly.

And know that you can surf again.

Care for yourself and give yourself what you need to nurture your body, mind and soul. Good nutrition. Time to relax and unwind. The chance to connect with those things that bring you joy.

Develop your inner strength and resilience.

And then, when the waves come, you won't drown in them. Instead, you'll surf on top of them, riding the waves with strength, inner peace and calm.

Mind Taming Peace Mantra:

I surf the waves of life.

49. Work with challenging emotions (aka what to do with anger)

I admit it. I can often feel angry.

Forget love and light; I often feel fury and fire.

Now, this may seem to contradict words I've written elsewhere in this book.

But bear with me — this is important!

Because there's a lot to be angry about in this world at the moment. And I feel it's important to recognise this so that we can transmute the energy of anger into action.

Misogyny and epidemic sexual harassment (yep #metoo).

People of colour being shot by police, victimised by those with power, and made to feel less-than by a white-centric culture.

Poverty, and a return to the insidious idea that poverty is somehow a moral failure rather than a result of widespread social injustice. That those in poverty are there through their own laziness or immorality and they should be penalised and stigmatised and made to feel shame to get measly handouts from the state.

The rich getting richer and thinking they deserve it, and they got all that money through their own hard work rather than benefiting from a system rigged in their favour.

Political classes who care more about party politics than the people they're meant to serve. Big pharma and the normalisation of pill-popping. Vested interests. Drugs. War. Terror. Global warming and environmental destruction.

Powerful people — usually angry white men in suits — are inflicting and condoning violence, destruction and hatred on our world.

It's easy to feel angry which soon becomes a frustrated sadness and a shoulder-shrugging impotence, and turning the other way.

No wonder mental health problems are on the rise. It's no surprise that depression and anxiety are at epidemic proportions.

If you have even half an ounce of empathy within you, then you can feel in your bones something is seriously out of alignment within the human race and this world.

And if you're sensitive to energy, then you can't escape the overwhelming stench of fear that pervades many Western cultures. You can feel the lies and manipulation and anger in your bones and frying your nervous system.

You're feeling pain because wounds are being inflicted every day: physical, emotional, cultural, mental, spiritual wounds.

I know. I feel it too. I feel angry and frustrated. It can feel deeply uncomfortable.

At the same time, we're fed the message that anger is something we shouldn't feel. Particularly in the personal development/self-help/spiritual and religious fields; in this arena of 'love and light' anger is frowned upon and looked down on.

There's an immense pressure to pretend that all is well and to sprinkle love, fairy dust and unicorns over everything to make it ok.

It's easy to succumb to the spiritual bypass with a love-bombing, 'ah we're all one so let's choose love and light', whitewash as if that's going to make the problems go away. (I hold my hand up to being guilty of that one in the past.)

But it's not and it won't.

And so, I feel angry — as a natural response to injustice.

If you feel this anger too then first, know you're not alone, and then, use it as a spur to action.

Something that happens in one country or to one person impact us all. Yes, in this respect we are all one. I believe that we are all, energetically, beings of light from the universal source, which is love. Trouble is, the human form we're in at the moment can inflict much pain on other living beings, so let's not pretend otherwise.

It's also easy to succumb to the fear; fear of the strength of feeling you may be experiencing. But fear will freeze you, make you close your eyes or look the other way. It will lead you to suppress the anger which will express itself in destructive ways such as snapping at your loved ones, or it will gnaw away inside you destroying your sense of self-esteem and connection to joy.

Instead, open up to the feelings of anger and reflect on their underlying message for you. What are you truly angry about? What is appalling you? What is in conflict with your deepest held values that is causing this anger?

Now see the anger as a call to action. To step up and make a difference.

Consider what you can do to be a good and decent human being and play your part in alleviating the pain in your incarnation in this precious, painfully beautiful human existence.

For some it might mean activism — speaking truth to power, intervening, bravely and fearlessly taking action (whether in your own family, workplace, local area or inter/nationally).

For others, it may mean healing your pain and fear so that you are conscious and loving and aware in your relationships; ensuring you won't pass your baggage onto the next generation.

Or supporting groups or individuals who are at the coalface of dealing with injustice.

Be brave. But please don't wear yourself out with guilt and anger. Do what lights you up and brings you joy, so you have the energy and vitality to show up in this world, for yourself, your loved ones, your community, and for those who don't have a voice whether through marginalisation or oppression.

Whatever path you take, choose it. Wake up. Live in alignment with your values. Don't look the other way and hope it will all go away. It won't. Don't ignore the anger. Don't deny that it is human to experience strong and challenging emotions. Don't force yourself to calm down and look the other way and tell yourself that you're powerless.

Let the anger burn within as a fire of transformation and let that fire transform your anger into conscious awareness and action. Root down into the core of your being and rise up to take positive action with your intentions, words and deeds. Each and every day.

Mind Taming Peace Mantra:

I transmute my challenging emotions

into positive action.

50. Feel ABLE to experience less stress and more peace

Do you ever feel at the mercy of the stress-filled myriad of thoughts rushing through your mind?

There's so much stuff rambling around in your brain that it tires you out! You can't seem to find an off-switch, but desperately wish you could.

You'd love to feel more peaceful, more positive and more present in your life, so you can enjoy simple pleasures and time with family and friends without that constant feeling of fretting and foreboding, which all too easily overshadows your daily life.

Yes? Well, all these things I've mentioned above have been my experience too — you're not alone! The vast majority of my yoga and meditation students come to me because they want to quieten their busy minds.

Brain overwhelm, and unsettled emotions are experienced by all of us. It comes with this fast-paced, stimulus-drenched, busy world in which we live.

Here are four simple steps to help you to press pause and get a handle on the thoughts and emotions that are troubling or overwhelming you.

I want to empower you to realise you are ABLE to tame your mind and feel more emotionally balanced.

The clue is in 'ABLE':

A-Accept
B-Breathe
L-Let it be
E-Enquire

Let's take each step in turn.

A – Accept: accept the feeling or thought

This idea might sound counter-intuitive. Accept feeling angry or fearful or anxious or scared or frustrated? But surely, I want these feelings to go away you might ask? Therein lies a problem!

So often we create more tension within ourselves by trying to push away strong feelings, painful emotions or troublesome thoughts.

We add salt to the wound by telling ourselves we shouldn't feel this way; we berate ourselves; we resist and struggle and add even more power to the emotional reactions.

In Buddhism, this is described as the Two Arrows. The first arrow that hits us is the pain of the thought or emotion. Then we hit ourselves with a second — even more painful — arrow (and third, fourth and fifth) with our reaction to the struggle, resistance and the dramatic stories we create in our minds.

Or, we push the feelings away or bottle up the emotions because we don't want to feel the grief or self-doubt or fear.

Ouch! That's a lot more emotional pain we're creating within ourselves.

For example, the same old record might play something like this: 'Oh, she criticised my work. Why? What does she know? She's such a know-it-all. Doesn't she realise how much work I put into that? Stupid cow! I don't know why I bother. I won't put so much work into it next time. Hmmm, perhaps it wasn't good enough in the first place. Oh, nothing I do seems good enough — here at work and at home. Everything I do seems to fail. I've got too much going on. I'm just no good. Oh God, I always get stuck in this self-doubt. Always! I wish I didn't feel this way. Why do I feel this way though? What's wrong with me?!'

Phew!

What would it feel like to change the record to this one instead? 'Oh, she criticised my work. Stupid cow! ... Oh OK, so I'm feeling angry and humiliated and doubtful' ... and then ...

B – Breathe
So simple but so powerful.

When you're feeling anxious, stressed, depressed or overwhelmed, your breathing will probably have become shallow, tight and fast.

Focus on the out-breath. Release some of the tension.

Let the inhale enter of its own accord (it will!). Breathe out slowly through your mouth and breathe in through your nose.

You're directly manipulating your nervous system here; when you exhale deeply and smoothly it sends a strong message back to your brain that you're safe and that you've got the situation under control.

Likely this will begin to diffuse the strong emotional reaction, so you can ...

L – Let it be: Can you just let the feelings be?
Can you sit with the anger, doubt or grief?

Stop pushing them away.

Release the struggle.

When we let go of the struggle; when we stop resisting how we feel, or we stop trying to get the mind to shut up, then waves of release can begin to wash through us.

In giving up the struggle, we let go on so many different levels.

The fists unclench, the jaw softens, the eyes relax, and the tightness in the head releases.
A fresh perspective can arise of its own accord.

Try it.

Practise surrendering to your busy mind. Give in to the fear and tension.

Let it be, and in doing so you'll diffuse the power of the grip of stressful thoughts and feelings, and you'll spontaneously feel more spacious and free.

And then you're in a better head space to ...

E – Enquire: What's the message for me here?
This idea is important and runs counter to the culture of positive thinking, which has a dangerous tendency to encourage us to bypass strong 'negative' emotions in favour of 'positive' emotions.

It's a recognition that our emotions are messengers. That anger, fear, doubt and shame are with us for a reason: to help us to learn.

It's a sense of 'opening the guest house' of your inner being to whatever guests show up, welcoming them in for tea and conversation so you can learn what they have to share.

There are two parts to this enquiry; ask yourself:

> 1. Where can I feel this emotion in my body? Is the fear showing up as butterflies in the stomach; is the frustration a tight jaw and clenched fists? Learn where the emotions show up. Breathe into them.

> 2. Why am I feeling this way? Is it a sign I need to change something in my life or something about this situation? Or do I need to accept the situation because I can't change it?

Or is it a sign to shift perspective — to learn to take responsibility for how I feel? To understand that while other people can trigger my feelings of low self-esteem or anger, the emotions are mine and mine alone to accept, enquire about and let go of? Or is it a habit — a button that's been pressed — and I've just spiralled off into a learned way of reacting?

In my personal experience, I have found that when I enquire into the messages behind the strong feelings and emotions, I will often discover patterns of behaviour, which have more to do with habitual reactions learned over the years, than what's going on in this moment!

So, with these four steps, you can reduce your emotional reactivity and learn to find more peace within yourself.

In accepting, breathing, letting it be and enquiring about what's really going on, you re-train your brain and balance the nervous system.

The mind becomes quieter. You'll let go of the emotional stress. You can shift your perspective. You'll become the witness of your inner landscape of thoughts and feelings and gradually become less at their mercy.

Mind Taming Peace Mantra:

I am ABLE to reduce stress and find peace within.

Shift Your Perspective

Thoughts in themselves are not bad. But when they get stuck on rigid expectations and judgements of how things should or shouldn't be, they become problematic. The same applies if we become enmeshed in pessimism or fear.

So, what's your take on your world and your life at the moment? What kind of thoughts are you regularly thinking? Nurturing and uplifting ones? Or thoughts that drag you down and add to your stress?

Are you aware of the deeply-held beliefs you're holding? About yourself? About the world?

Because those beliefs are shaping how you perceive your reality.

Do you view life through the lens of love or the prison-bars of fear?

Now, we all have challenging stuff in our lives, and we all have emotional baggage.

Similarly, we can all think of something we feel grateful for. It's all about perspective.

It can take a while to shift, but it's worth the effort.

As human beings we often get ingrained in our beliefs and habits and mistake them for facts and the truth.

And when we come down to it, thinking, and the nature of our thoughts is often at the root cause of anxiety, as well as other strong emotions such as anger, doubt and jealousy.

We might not be aware of this because often thinking is beneath our conscious level of awareness. The thoughts babble away, and we're hardly aware of them.

The kind of thoughts that fuel these strong emotions often relate to feelings of unworthiness; of not being good enough; that somehow, we're flawed human beings.

The key to dealing with this?

Shift your perceptive to know that you are not your thoughts.

You are not the things you say or think. This concept can be difficult to get your head around!

It means being aware of the mental chatter and seeing it for what it is: chatter, habits of thinking, and judgments that perhaps once helped you and kept you 'safe', but are now no longer needed.

In this section, I'll share with you guidance and practices that aim to shift your way of thinking. To empower you to realise that you are not at the mercy of events, challenges, other people — or your mind.

Shifting your perspective is all about harnessing the power of the mind so you can learn to focus your mind, your energy and your willpower to live a life of greater joy and peaceful presence.

*

51. Choose your thoughts wisely

Never underestimate the power of the thoughts you think and the language you use in your thinking to shape how you experience yourself and your life.

Positive affirmations (statements in the present tense positively affirming how you wish to feel such as 'I am peaceful'; 'I have all the support I need') can help to retrain the brain and to choose where you place your focus.

Have you tried them? And if so, have you found your mind struggles and resists? Sometimes? Always?

The trick is to keep repeating them anyway. The conscious mind might resist, but the unconscious mind hears the words. It takes whatever you think about as the literal truth.

For this reason, it's important to wrest back control from your worrying, judging monkey mind and put some intention into your thoughts.

You're re-programming the brain to think differently.

Try beginning your affirmations with 'I choose to …' rather than 'I am …' as this can cause less friction in your mind and lets you open to the possibility that the intention can be, or is, true for you.

So, here are some of my favourite affirmations. Give them a try and see how they land with you.

Breathe, repeat silently and/or out loud.

'*I love and approve of myself just as I am.*'
'*I am me, and I am free.*'
'*I am grounded. I am safe. I am supported.*'

(Remember, if you feel resistant to them, try beginning them with 'I choose to …' or 'I choose to feel that …' instead.)

What would you like to create in your life?

What positive qualities would you like to cultivate?

Write them down now: beginning with, 'I am ...' or 'I choose to ...'

Write them on post-it notes and plaster them around your house.

Repeat, daily, as many times as you can — and then a few more!

Whatever you say and think, your subconscious mind takes as the literal truth.

So choose your thoughts wisely.

If your thoughts are all 'meh' and negativity, you'll experience the world as an indifferent and negative place.

Focus with enthusiasm and commitment to living your life, and that energy will come back to you in abundance.

Make the cycle of energy a virtuous circle by committing to whatever you're doing in any given moment.

Because your thoughts shape your reality.

Mind Taming Peace Mantra:

My thoughts create my perception of reality.

52. Watch where your energy goes

Energy flows where your attention goes...

Thinking that the world is unjust, and having thoughts that, 'people like me aren't successful', or, 'I'll never live the life I want'; will likely mean that's what you'll experience. (Those are thoughts I used to think btw.)

It's like you're experiencing the world with an 'everything-is-shitty' filter - so that's what you'll see and experience.

Now, I'm not talking about going around Pollyanna-style pretending everything is sweetness and light (it's not, there is a lot of pain and injustice in the world as well as much kindness and love).

It's about tending to your own mind and noticing how this affects your day-to-day life experience and interactions.

Noticing the tone of your thoughts and checking in with whether they're helping you or hindering you.

Then choosing whether this is how you really want to think and experience the world.

Do you want to get stuck in problems or focus your energy on finding solutions?

I'm not judging you either way.

But realise, you DO have a choice.

Mind Taming Peace Mantra:

I choose which thoughts to give my energy to.

53. Ask if it's real

I love these words from Mark Twain: *'I have known a great many troubles in my life — but most of them never happened'.*

Ha! This is SO true!

How many of your troubles are mind-made?

The mind loves to worry, to fret, to prepare for the worst, to catastrophize, to dramatize. It's all part of the body-mind's deep-seated survival instinct.

But you don't have to be at the mercy of your worries. You can learn to choose whether the troubles need your attention or are mind-made.

Practise discerning between what is a fact and what is something your mind has made up or put its own dramatic spin on — learn to judge well.

Practise checking in with your thoughts daily and ask, 'Is this real? Or is it my fearful mind trying to trick me?'.

And if it's your fears talking, smile gently to yourself and tell your mind, 'Thank you, I know you're just trying to look out for me, but I don't need to listen to this today'.

And breathe and let it go.

Mind Taming Peace Mantra:

I watch my thoughts and understand

they're just my perception of what I'm experiencing.

54. Be the sovereign of your inner world

No-one can rule your inner world except you.

Did you know that?

Can you feel that?

This is such an important realisation.

How many times have you said, 'she made me so angry', 'he upset me' and so on? (Yup, me too!)

Truth: No-one can make you feel or think anything unless you choose to let them.

This can be a difficult lesson to learn. It means taking responsibility.

It means being courageous enough to look within and feel what you're feeling rather than numbing it out.

It means owning your emotions and thoughts.

But it also means liberation from the constant merry-go-round of being pulled this way and that by life and other people, and their own baggage.

(And it also means recognising that other people's stuff and baggage belongs to them, not you!)

So, whenever you're feeling reactive, frustrated, angry, down on yourself — look within.

With a kind, generous and wise heart ask yourself: 'do I wish to feel this way?', 'why am I feeling this way?'.

Am I reacting to someone else? Am I letting life push my buttons?

And decide how you would like to feel instead.

Let go of what you don't need. Choose your attitude.

Choose your thoughts.

Practise. Persist.

Re-programme your mental habits.

Take control of your inner landscape.

Wake up and find freedom.

Mind Taming Peace Mantra:

I choose to take control of my inner world.

55. Start your day with intention

Here's a question for you. What's your intention for today? Did you answer something along the lines of, 'Erm, dunno'? Or, 'Just get through it?'

Daily life can all too easily turn into a hamster wheel of: get up; go to work or look after the kids or run around all day doing stuff; arrive home exhausted; flop in front of the TV; haul yourself off to bed before repeating it all the next day.

We're so busy, busy, busy — in a culture that unhealthily glorifies 'busy' and habitual productivity — that one day can easily feel like the next.

Events determine what we experience each day and how we feel.

What would it feel like to know there's another way?

Imagine living each day with purpose and intention.

Yes, you might still need to do the same stuff, but what if you no longer needed to feel pulled this way and that as if you had no control over what you do and how you feel?

This is the gift that the power of intention offers us.

Your mind shapes the way you experience life.

If your mind is all over the place and unfocused, you'll feel pulled this way and that in all that you do.

If your mind dwells in the past, you will find it difficult to approach the future with confidence.

If your mind is always jumping forward anticipating all the 'what ifs' of any given situation, you will find it impossible to enjoy what you have, here, in your life now.

Working with intentions gives the subconscious mind a focus and will help you to create a radiant life.

Begin at the start of the day.

What are the first thoughts and feelings you have on waking?

Maybe the to-do list starts running; you dread a difficult appointment you've got coming up; worries and fretting start whirring around your head. Or perhaps it's just a generalised feeling of 'ugh, another day to battle through'.

What would it feel like to begin the day with an intention of how you would like to experience the day?

Maybe you'd like courage, or serenity, acceptance or calm. Then start the day feeling this.

Before you even get up. Take some deep breaths and decide how you are going to experience today. How you are going to approach it.

Today I am calm.
Today I am courageous.
Today I am serene.
Today I am efficient and focused.
Today I accept what life brings me.
Today I am grateful for the lessons I shall learn.

Use the present tense: that's vital to trick your mind into feeling it to be real, now.

Then get out of bed and make it part of your morning routine to stand (or sit) upright and feel strong yet relaxed. Take some deep breaths.

Visualize the day unfolding according to your affirmation. What actions will you take? What thoughts will you think? What will you do? What won't you do?

Write down your intention and put it where you can see it. See it, feel it. And then notice if this creates a shift in your experience of daily life.

You always have a choice.

Set a positive intention each day and it will help you cope with what life brings you.

It will help you live life with joy and ease in your heart.

Mind Taming Peace Mantra:

I choose how I experience each day

with my focus and intention.

56. Find the space between stimulus and response

How many times do your buttons get pushed each day?

Someone cuts you up on the drive to work and you swear at them, and your blood boils.

A colleague keeps chattering when you're trying to concentrate. Perhaps you snap at them, or you wind yourself up silently berating them.

You see a post on social media and start comparing your life to that person's and you begin to feel inadequate.

There are a million and one ways our emotionally reactive buttons can get pressed every day.

Each time we allow our buttons to get pressed we add to our levels of stress and tension and anxiety.

But you don't have to react.

Read that again. You have a choice. You don't have to react.

Much of our reactivity is based on habit.

So, choose to develop a new habit.

Breathe. Pause. Make a conscious decision about how to act rather than blindly reacting.

The more we do this — and reduce our habitual unhelpful reactions — the more we create new positive habits by rewiring the brain to react differently. We start to train ourselves to live in and act from a space of equilibrium.

A great way to do this is to tune into your breath. And, as your breath naturally slows down, notice the little pause of stillness and peace at the end of the in-breath, and again at the end of the out-breath.

Tune into that peace and stillness each day.

Then when someone or something presses your buttons, you'll slowly begin to notice that you no longer react. You breathe. Slow down. You choose how to respond.

Therein lies your growth and your freedom.

Mind Taming Peace Mantra:

I mindfully choose how I respond to life

each and every day.

57. Change your life with these little words

I'd like to introduce you to five tiny words, which have the power to transform your life and the way you think and feel about your circumstances.

Five little words, which remind you to let go of wishing things were different.

Five little words, which bring acceptance and peace.

Five little words, which when used regularly can change your life.

What are they?

'*It is as it is.*'

How many times a day do you tell yourself something shouldn't be this way or should be that way?

You slept through your alarm clock. OK, that's inconvenient but beating yourself up isn't going to turn back time. It is as it is.

Your partner left the kitchen in a mess after making their breakfast. Again. Shouting at them or running a story in your head about how lazy they are, isn't going to clear up the crumbs. It is as it is.

You get stuck in a traffic jam on the way to work. Getting angry and frustrated isn't going to move the traffic any quicker. It is as it is.

And so it goes on ...

Let go of the striving and pain.

If circumstances, habits, thoughts or behaviours need to change to improve the flow of your life, then set your intention to make the changes you need, and then take action.

But, the here and now? Well, it is as it is.

Mind Taming Peace Mantra:

It is as it is.

Peace Lies Within

58. Accept this moment

Practise this beautiful meditation to encourage a sense of acceptance of what you are experiencing here in this moment.

You can listen to a guided version in the resources which accompany this book.

Meditation on Acceptance

1. Sit comfortably and take some deep, soothing breaths.

2. Notice the sounds around you ... accept any sounds you hear as part of this present moment.

AFFIRM: *I accept my environment.*

3. Notice any sensations in your body ... try not to judge them ... accept them ... they are all part of this perfect, present moment.

AFFIRM: *I accept my body and how it is in this moment.*

4. Notice any thoughts that arise ... is your mind trying to distract you? ... Let the thoughts go ... notice ... observe. Don't allow yourself to be drawn into them ... it's your choice.

AFFIRM: *I accept my mind.*

And take this practice out into your life every day.

Mind Taming Peace Mantra:

I accept my environment. I accept my body.

I accept my mind.

134

59. Choose freedom

So often we get lost in the 'what ifs' and 'shoulds' or 'shouldn'ts' of our life experience.

We wish things had been different. We let our past shape our present and our future.

What if we could let go of those stories?

What if we decided to learn the useful lessons from our past and then let it go?

What if we decided consciously to choose to shape our future?

What if we decided to live in the present?

What if we chose to live free of the past and the future?

Then we'd become very powerful indeed!

Move your body to let go of past emotions and old, stagnant energy that is stuck in your muscles and joints.

Breathe deeply. Relax.

Do things that help you to feel physically freer, and you will find that the mental blocks and emotional ties begin to loosen and release. Whether that's through yoga, swimming, running, walking, gardening or dancing. Do it!

Do things which enable you to step into, and experience, the present moment and the power of stillness, whether that's meditation, gazing at clouds, working with crafts or painting. Do it.

And smile.

Live in the present. Let go of the past. Stop fretting about the future.

Realise that when you're fully present, you have the power to shape your life and to actually experience, and live your life!

And with this presence, you become powerful and free (which is what you were all along but had maybe forgotten).

Mind Taming Peace Mantra:

I am powerful, and I am free.

60. Use the power of your sense of smell

There's a technique in Neuro-Linguistic Programming (NLP) called 'Anchoring'. (NLP is a bit like the user manual for your brain helping you to get in charge of your thoughts and feelings.)

Anchoring is used to induce a particular frame of mind or emotion, such as happiness or relaxation; a state. It usually involves a touch, gesture or word as an 'anchor'. You use and reuse it, and your brain then begins to make an automatic connection between that act or word, and the state you've associated with it.

It's a bit like the feeling you get when you lie down for your relaxation at the end of a yoga class. Over time your brain has been trained to know what's coming. So, the simple act of lying down on your yoga mat can start to activate the state of relaxation.

Our senses can help us create anchors to deal with overwhelm, stress and anxiety. Listening to a particular piece of music that calms us, for example, or looking at a picture of a place or person that makes us feel content and happy.

But there's one sense, which is particularly powerful.

The sense of smell.

It's the only sense directly linked to the parts of the brain responsible for emotions, memory and survival instincts; the parts that tag events with emotions creating deep and strong unconscious memories.

It's why the sense of smell seems to uniquely and strangely take us straight back to an event or memory in a visceral way.

A smell can take us straight back to childhood. The strong smell of tomatoes on the vine takes me back to my nan's greenhouse where she grew them!

So, we can use this to our benefit.

Research shows that particular scents affect our brains and can alter our mood-state in specific ways.

Floral scents — such as lavender or rose — have calming effects. Tree, herb and grass scents have a grounding and soothing effect. Mint, citrus and spicy scents can have a powerfully energising, uplifting and warming effect.

So, if we choose a scent, or blend of scents, which induce a preferred mood-state, we can use that as an anchor in everyday life to shift us out of negative thought and feeling habits.

We use the inherent links between the scents and feeling-states to proactively bring about how we wish to feel.

We train the brain to associate the smell with a particular feeling. Add in some positive affirmations, and you've got a very powerful tool for emotional health and wellbeing.

When you feel over-stimulated or stressed, keep some lavender essential oil on you and take a sniff when you need to throughout the day. Or mix it with carrier oil and apply it to your skin. **AFFIRM:** *I relax into peace.*

If you're feeling jittery and ungrounded, you could inhale a scent, which is known to have a grounding effect, such as clary sage, frankincense or patchouli. **AFFIRM:** *I am grounded, safe and secure.*

If you're feeling tired and lethargic, inhaling peppermint or citrus scents such as lemon, orange or grapefruit can uplift you. **AFFIRM:** *I am awake and full of abundant energy.*

Connect to your sense of smell. Breathe deeply and smoothly. Notice the physical feelings the experience of the smell brings about in your body. Maybe feelings of tension melting away. Feeling the ground beneath your feet. Feeling zingy and awake.

Soon enough just smelling the scent will activate the feeling. You'll become more present and the real you will emerge: joyful, loving, present and enthusiastic. You'll drop anchor into calmer waters!

So, remember to come to your senses and come into this moment.

Mind Taming Peace Mantra:

I create positive anchors to bring me home to now.

61. Dance as though no-one is watching you

Do you sometimes find that there's something stopping you from trying new things; from overcoming obstacles; from speaking up; or from doing something a little crazy or out of your comfort zone?

Have you ever asked yourself what it is that's stopping you?

I propose there's one thing common to us all that holds us back: fear.

OK, if you're faced with a situation where your physical or emotional safety could be compromised, fear is probably a healthy reaction.

But beyond that, fear becomes debilitating.

What's making you scared?

Fear is often about being frightened that we're going to be judged, criticised or laughed at by others. That we won't fit in. That we're not good enough.

But why fear? Because our ego is driving this reaction. Our ego-mind is telling us we should be perfect, that we're better than everyone else. The fear comes from the thought that we might fail to prove ourselves to be superior to those around us.

So our fear of being criticised may stem from our ego telling us that we're better than everyone else! The mind is a funny thing. You've got to laugh at yourself; right?

Does this make sense to you?

Think of an example when you stopped yourself from doing something because that voice in your head said you couldn't do it or that you'd look stupid. What were you scared of? Why? What was the worst that could have happened? Why would it have mattered if you'd 'failed'? What is 'looking stupid' anyway?

Is there an element of pride or vanity or ego in your answers?

So how do we deal with this ego-driven fear?

We notice it and name it.

Awareness is the light that we can shine into the deepest elements of our self to be able to see and understand what is driving us.

We need courage and discipline to do this, but it's worth it. We need to show ourselves some love and acceptance.

And to be OK with whatever we experience.

This helps us to get in touch with our thoughts and encourages us to be aware of their effects.

And this connects us to an inner, silent observer who can name the thoughts without getting pulled along by them.

Creating space for us to choose how to act rather than continuously repeating cycles of unhealthy reactions.

Ultimately, we can begin to see and understand for ourselves that we are guided by two basic instincts: fear and love.

Fear leads us to separation — from our self and others.

Love leads us to connection — to our inner wisdom, to each other and to a sense of infinite love that binds all living things.

Connect to your inner guide and choose love.

So, here's an example of a time when I over-rode my ego's voice and did what I wanted; with joy.

A few years ago now, I was at a party organised by my workplace. A live folk band was playing some of the music I love. My foot was tapping all night, my shoulders dancing.

Apart from the set dances, nobody was getting up to freewheel and go for it. I was itching to get up and throw some moves on the empty dance floor. But something kept stopping me. All those eyes watching me. What if they thought I looked like a prat?

Then it came to the last set of the evening. And I thought, sod it! I love to dance. I'm going for it!

So I did. I got up and danced with a massive smile on my face, feeling totally alive, and completely in the flow of that moment. Even with a whole room of people watching me.

And I loved it despite the people watching me. OK, all right then, it was also fun because I let my inner show-off shine through.

I let myself be me.

But when I got home, a little voice appeared that caused me to feel embarrassed that I'd done it, that people thought I was silly, looked stupid, was drunk, was a show-off, was conceited.

Then a deeper intuition noticed this fear-driven voice and said, 'that's OK. Even if anyone did think that, does it matter? No-one was hurt'.

I'd followed my instinct to move; to be joyful; to enjoy the moment; to feel the music and express it in the most natural way possible. I felt in love with life. And it felt so much better than to leave off doing something for worry about what others might think.

So, dance as though no-one is watching you.

Show true courage and strength.

Live your life with love and joy.

Mind Taming Peace Mantra:

I choose to live my life with joy.

62. Spread an inner smile

Practise this **Inner Smile Meditation** to spread calm contentment into every cell of your being.

You can listen to a guided version in the resources which accompany this book.

1. Sit comfortably ... breathe steadily and let the breath become calm and peaceful.

2. Take yourself back to a memory ... a time when you were intensely happy ... as you relive this experience feel a gentle smile of happiness spread across your face.

3. Now take this smile to your eyes ... making them sparkle behind your closed eyelids.

4. Feel a warm glow develop as your smile expands to fill your whole body ... from your forehead ... down the back of your head ... through your neck. Feel your shoulders smiling ... and feel the smiles spreading down your arms and into your hands.

5. Feel the inner smile filling your organs ... let your waist smile ... your hips are smiling ... smiles spread down your legs and into your feet.

6. Finally let this inner smile fill your heart and just sit in your body joyfully smiling, and affirm to yourself: *I accept myself, just as I am, right now.*

Mind Taming Peace Mantra:

I accept myself, just as I am, right now.

63. Cut the cords

Is there someone in your life who gets under your skin?

Perhaps a family member or a colleague?

Someone who irks you just thinking about them. Or someone you keep comparing yourself to. Or someone who seems to leave you feeling drained, stressed, anxious or fed-up.

Thinking about them or being around them knocks you off emotional balance.

I think we all have someone in our life like this.

So, what to do?

First off, realise it's not really about them, it's about YOU.

Ouch!

Did that hurt?

Look, I know that some people seem to be born awkward, annoying, close-minded.

But if we're honest about it, it's our reaction to them that is causing us the issues.

You can't change these people.

You can only change your reaction to them.

Your thoughts and your perceptions of them are messing with your mind and your emotions. You've allowed them to get entangled in your energy like they have tentacles hooked into you.

It's time to cut yourself free!

Try this powerful visualisation to release these unhealthy, energetic and emotional ties. (There's a recording you can follow in the resources which accompany this book.)

Sit comfortably and close your eyes or lower your gaze.

In your mind's eye, imagine you are in a place where you feel safe and secure. Imagine yourself sitting there.

Whether it's a room, an imaginary place or somewhere outside.

It's your place. And no-one can come there unless you allow them.

When you're ready — and at your invitation — imagine a person who causes you issues walking slowly towards you. Tell them to stop at whatever distance you're happy for them to be in relation to you.

And you begin to see cords, ties, tentacles coming from this person's body, attaching themselves to you. And you have cords, ties and tentacles coming from your body attaching you to them.

Notice where they attach to you, and where they're coming from.

Breathe.

You are safe.

Just notice where you feel the attachment to this person. And don't forget the back of your body too.

Now feel that you are holding a sword of light in your hand … pure light … golden and glowing.

And when you're ready, use the sword to cut these ties that bind the two of you together.

Cut and release these cords. With large, swooping movements or quick sudden chops.

Feel the cords loosening and dropping away.

Keep cutting them until they have all dropped away from both of you to the floor. See them melting into the floor. You are free.

Now thank this person who is standing in front of you.

Thank them for the lessons they have taught you.

And then notice them turn and walk away — to continue to live their life.

And now you are free to live yours; liberated from the ties that had been binding the two of you together and draining your energy.

Feel yourself light and free. Strong and open.

Phew. What a relief!

Mind Taming Peace Mantra:

I release the energetic ties to people

who I find difficult and challenging.

64. Don't judge a fish by its ability to climb a tree

... to paraphrase Einstein!

Now, we've all at some time been given the message that we're not good enough, we're not doing something right, or we don't fit in.

I spent years working in jobs that eroded my self-esteem, and sat in many a meeting beating myself up because I wasn't speaking up. Now I realise that I was a wonderful fish trying to climb a tree. That environment was never going to be the place for me to shine.

Where are you a fish trying to climb a tree? What areas of your life do you feel out of alignment with who you truly are? What do you need to shift, rebalance or change so you can walk YOUR path?

We all have something. Whether it's work or a relationship or the face we present to the world.

If it's not in alignment with who we really are and what we truly need in our lives at this moment, there'll be a niggling feeling that something is out of kilter.

It can feel challenging to change — but it IS possible.

It took me a few years, but I eventually left the workplaces that dimmed my light and decided to walk my path — to swim in my river to extend the fish analogy — and let me, be me.

So, stop trying to climb that tree if you're a fish! Be you. Love and appreciate yourself. Walk YOUR path.

Mind Taming Peace Mantra:

I choose to walk my path with ease and grace.

65. Live life your way

Why oh why does our culture glorify busy-ness so much? It seems we're supposed to struggle; to push through our comfort zones; to do; to achieve; to climb the ladder. Blah, blah, blimmin' blah. Whatevs.

Some would have you believe that unless you're jumping out of aeroplanes; hiking up mountains; busting a gut to climb the ladder of life; learning to stand on your head and generally grabbing at every sensation-filled opportunity then you're somehow letting life pass you by.

We're not meant to want to relax in calm contentment.

Well, do you know what? I can't be bothered. It all sounds way too overwhelming and tiring for me.

I'm not lazy. I work hard and yes, I find myself pushing too (and wind up exhausted when I do). For me, life is for savouring. For appreciating the beauties around us. For finding joy in simple pleasures. For noticing the details others may miss.

Living life to the full, for me, is gazing at flowers; spending time with loved ones; time on my yoga mat; eating cake; hugging trees; watching the sun go down over the horizon while sipping a glass of something lovely; basking in the light of a full moon and for staring at clouds.

Delighting in the simple pleasures of the senses through light, and scents, and sounds and subtle vibes. And always looking up and noticing what's around me.

Life is for living with a sense of joy, gratitude and contentment.

Mind Taming Peace Mantra:

I live life, my way.

66. Get solar powered

When you're feeling tired and your head's all over the place, or if you need a boost of energy and willpower, use this **Solar Meditation** to harness the power of your mind and intention to fill yourself with solar energy.

There's a recording of this in the resources which accompany this book.

Take as long as you need or as much time as you have.

> 1. Sit comfortably … Lengthen through your spine … breathe and let the breath settle, becoming steady.
>
> 2. First, notice the solid ground beneath you, and let the earth support you.
>
> 3. Then tune into the air around … the air that gives you life.
>
> 4. Now imagine a beam of golden sunlight shining down onto the crown of your head … a beam of sunlight … just for you … vibrant … full of life and energy.
>
> 5. And draw that light down through the crown your head … breathe it in and down into your Solar Plexus (upper abdominal area). Breathing out, feel an inner glow begin to build.
>
> 6. Sit for a few moments and continue to breathe in that golden, shimmering life force … that wonderful energy … down into your solar plexus. Let yourself be filled up with all the light, healing and energy you need.
>
> 7. Then, after a few minutes, send that energy to any place within you that feels like it needs it … any place within you that feels tired, or weak or aching. Send strength … healing … love … whatever you need.

8. And then sit quietly for a few more moments.

9. Finally, let the light from your Solar Plexus rise to your heart ... and let that warmth and light fill your heart. Your heart becomes golden and radiant and filled with love.

And know that you have all you need inside yourself.

Mind Taming Peace Mantra:

I have all the resources I need within me

to achieve my dreams.

67. Try a new perspective

Perspective.

Such a wonderful gift.

That sense of accepting what you can't change and taking action to change what you can. And truly seeing the difference.

But how can we attain it?

Well, begin by examining the areas you are struggling with in life.

Something to do with your health? Your wealth? Your job? Your relationships?

Stand back and try to look at it from a different perspective — as an impartial observer.

What could you truly do to change the situation? What do you not really need to endure? Take the steps you need.

If the situation can't be 'cured' what can you do to lessen your suffering around it? How can you learn to 'endure' it, to make peace with it?

Breathe, sit in stillness with this. And listen to what your heart tells you. Trust your inner wisdom to guide you

(Tip: if you feel fearful, that's your head speaking!).

Mind Taming Peace Mantra:

When I feel stuck,

I look at the issue from a different perspective.

68. Reclaim calm

'Oh, she's got so much energy!' 'Ooh, I don't know how she does it all!' 'Gosh, I wish I had her energy!'

How many times have you said that and felt a pang of envy, or a kick of inadequacy in comparison?

I know I have.

Some people seem to pack their lives full of activities and achievements. They have a hundred plates spinning at any given time. They are popular and always smiling. Their home is immaculate.

'Oh crap, I wish I was like that! Why do I feel like I need a nap some afternoons? Am I wasting time watching the birds or pootling in the garden or curling up to read?'

It's all too easy to let those thoughts into your mind which fester, and you get stuck in comparisonitis.

I've been there and can easily still go there.

But then I take a moment to reflect.

Why do we glorify being busy?

Why is appearing to have so much energy, and be doing all-the-things something we envy?

I have a different perspective on this I'd like to share.

We live in a culture addicted to 'busy'. We have career ladders to climb. Bigger houses to buy. Lots of Joneses to keep up with.

Governments and the media are obsessed with (unsustainable) economic growth (hey, the planet's not getting any bigger, haven't they noticed?).

Success is measured by achievement, attainment and buying more, more, more!

And on an individual level, many of us know deep down this is an empty and unsustainable way to live. So we numb ourselves and play along with the prevalent culture.

'Keep yourself busy. Keep a lid on those uncomfortable feelings!'

So, that person who seems to have so much energy? Yes, maybe she's an extrovert who loves being around people, or perhaps she likes to feel she's developing and achieving and growing and gets a lot of self-esteem from that.

Or maybe she's internalised our culture's addiction to busy and feels she's failing unless she's constantly doing and achieving. Maybe she's keeping herself so busy so as not to address worries in her life and/or is numbing out uncomfortable feelings; possibly, she's on her way to burn-out.

The reality is probably a murky mix of all of the above, with a few more issues thrown in for good measure.

I'm not saying having lots of energy and making the most of life is a bad thing.

Not at all.

Enjoy life. Live life.

But if you find yourself addicted to being busy or envying others their jam-packed life, then I invite you to honestly ask yourself, why?

Does this busy-ness truly delight you? Or is it a habit? Or is it something you think you should do?

And I also invite us all to acknowledge that human beings need rest.

We need downtime. Our body and mind need to rest and restore.

Admittedly perhaps some of us need more rest than others. I need PLENTY otherwise I end up a confusing combination of totally wired and bone-tired. (#highlysensitiveperson)

We need time to ourselves and time to connect meaningfully with others.

And there's nothing wrong with that.

There's nothing wrong with taking your time. Focusing on one thing at a time. Doing what brings you joy rather than what brings you kudos. Filling up your well rather than draining it dry. Taking time to savour the small pleasures in life rather than missing life as it whizzes past in a blur.

Trouble is the slow and simple life is out of kilter with our materialistic, economic growth-obsessed, planet-trashing culture, so we're made to feel we're not contributing enough.

Well, I for one see that for what is. Junk values; making money for the already rich.

I'm happy to swim against that tide, thank you.

So, I choose no longer to play that game of envying people who appear to be full of energy and achieving loads, and who are probably stuck in the prevailing consumerist culture.

I'm quite content to take the slow road. To watch and listen, reflect and learn. And then to share and connect with others from a meaningful depth of experience.

So, if like me, you feel alienated and out of place in our busy, noisy, often unkind, over-stimulating culture, please know you're not alone.

I'm with you, and I'm standing up for those of us who are gentler, sensitive souls who appreciate and revel in, and are lit up by, the simple and gentle beauties of life!

We only have one life in this body at this time.

Say 'thanks, but no thanks' to the hustle, and pressure, and judgmentalism of our prevailing culture.

So, here's my alternative approach to life; a manifesto for calm contentment, if you will.

1. Stand up for slowness, gentleness, kindness, sensitivity.

2. Know that self-care is not selfish. It's essential for your physical and mental wellbeing.

3. Practise daily gratitude. Be content with what you already have in your life, and who you are now.

4. Make time to relax; seek out opportunities to calm your nervous system.

5. Do what brings you joy.

6. Appreciate the simple pleasures in life.

7. Let go of the fear of missing out; let go of comparison and competition.

8. Choose your thoughts wisely.

9. Meditate daily in whatever way works for you so you can connect to stillness.

10. Love and accept yourself. Know you ARE enough.

Mind Taming Peace Mantra:

I slow down and savour life.

69. Breathe to empowerment

All too often we can feel like our life is out of our control.

Whether it's in the workplace; our family; our health; or the wider issues of social and economic and environmental changes in our world.

And, we're also trained to look outside ourselves for what we need to feel happy and content — and enough.

This creates a toxic mix of fear of lack, and a sense of powerlessness to do anything about it.

I'd like to share with you a powerful technique to remind you, and to help you feel that, you have an abundance of energy and resources within YOU. You don't need to look elsewhere for confirmation.

It reminds you that you have all the inner resources you need: willpower, love, strength, compassion, curiosity, wisdom. It's all there ready to be tapped into.

This simple but powerful breathing technique will help to build a sense of inner power, and a belief that you are in the driving seat of your life: **The Empowerment Breath**.

Practise it each morning and see the difference it makes to your life!

1. Sit or kneel in an upright position.

2. Breathe in as you bring your hands, palms together, in front of the centre of your chest.

3. Breathe out, extending your arms forward, turn the palms outwards and keep the tips of the index fingers and thumbs together to form a triangle.

4. Take a deep in-breath.

5. On the out-breath make the sound 'ssssss' taking your arms out to the sides and then down towards the ground. Feel the expansion in the area of your chest. **AFFIRM**: *I believe in myself. I am in control of my life. I have all the inner resources I need.*

And invite in the fact that you are powerful. You are courageous. You are strong.

Feel it in every cell of your being; allow this knowledge to sink into your bones.

Empower yourself!

Mind Taming Peace Mantra:

I believe in myself. I am in control of my life.

I have all the inner resources I need.

70. Don't be nice

Be calm. Be grounded. But don't feel you have to be nice!

Please, don't mistake being grounded and calm for being a nice, good girl or boy, or a push-over!

If, like me, you're sensitive to the emotions of others and their moods and energies, you may find it all too easy to ignore and suppress your own needs and feelings.

We can become a people-pleaser through fear of feeling that raw sense of the disapproval of others if we don't do what they want. We tangibly feel their disapproval as our nervous systems pick up on the vibes they give out and we get overwhelmed with shame, guilt and anxiety at this physically perceived disapproval.

This need to avoid overwhelm can lead us to want to say and do the 'right thing' all the time. It can feel easier than dealing with not meeting the expectations of others.

I'm bored of being 'nice' and the 'good' girl and saying and doing the 'right thing'. No, I'm not playing that game anymore.

My first yoga teacher, Mary, frequently shared her take on 'nice' as an acronym, and it always made me chuckle as it struck a chord. **NICE: Nasty Interior Cheerful Exterior.**

There's nothing wrong with being amenable, courteous and helpful.

But if — by being 'nice', and calm and Zen — we're stifling words that need to come out, or if we're going along with actions or ways of being, which aren't in accord with our own needs and our true selves, then we're lying to ourselves.

We're oppressing ourselves. We're creating conflict, tension and resistance within ourselves. We're not honouring our own needs.

We're creating stress within our bodies through the actions of our minds.

Because what's pushed down will eventually come up and burst out; whether through anger or illness. I don't want to be a pushover. And I don't want to be angry or ill either!

Which, for me, is where the practice of grounding, calming and relaxation comes in.

Grounding and being calm, *not* nice and floaty and eager to please. Be present, still and strong.

When you're grounded, you notice the anxiety but know you can let it go.

You learn to see what's causing it. Maybe it's an over-stimulating loud and busy work environment. Maybe it's because you're pushing yourself to conform to having a full social life when what you crave most is some peaceful, quiet, me-time. Maybe you're picking up on the moods of others causing you to feel anxious for no reason.

And when you're grounded, you can see when something needs to change, and you can move beyond the fear of the reaction you may get should you choose to express your needs.

So, stand or sit in stillness and ground yourself and repeat these statements:

I ground and feel the physical strength in my legs and core and my spine.

I ground and access the support of the strong, stable, nourishing Earth beneath me.

I ground and allow my inner strength, resolve, courage and creativity to arise within me.

I ground and let go of excess nervous tension and anxiety to be calm, and endeavour to act with awareness, rather than react from habit or having my buttons pressed.

I stand my ground and give myself what I need: quiet-time, space to think, time to breathe and release and allow and receive.

I ground myself and calm my nervous system and quieten my busy mind, to allow the voice of my intuition, my higher self to whisper her teachings.

My higher self knows the way forward. S/he knows what is best for me.

Ground. Breathe. Root.

Listen to your own needs. Let your voice speak.

Rise up to shine your unique light to the world.

Mind Taming Peace Mantra:

I root. I rise.

71. Call back your power

Do you feel your power? Do you feel in control of your life? Do you feel completely happy in your skin?

If the answer is 'no' to any of these questions, then please know you're not alone.

Low self-esteem is rife in our society (particularly amongst sensitive people who've had a lifetime of people telling them not to be so emotional, to get over it, and to grow a thicker skin).

Feeling crap about yourself in some way is a hidden epidemic and a taboo subject as it's rarely talked about. Who wants to admit to feeling this way?

It's contributing towards the high levels of stress and anxiety and mental health issues in our society.

There are many and complex factors contributing to feelings of low self-worth from upbringing, schooling and life experience, to what you put into your body/mind through food and media.

But there's a clear thread in the messages we're fed through the media and advertising that deeply contributes to this: the message that you're broken, and you need fixing.

It's a truth that we live in a world where a lot of people make a lot of money from telling us we're broken, and that if we buy their product it will make us feel better and fix us.

We're bombarded with subtle, insidious messages hundreds, if not thousands, of times a day.

It's bound to wear you down!

And sometimes personal development and spiritual teachings can compound that. 'Buy this book, do this course, follow this practice to be a better person.'

So, how do we deal with all of this without letting it erode our spirit and soul?

You can call back your power by feeding your inner strength, practising being present and choosing how to feel in order to reveal what was already there: your beautiful human soul; your inner wisdom; your infinite power.

Spiritual practices such as yoga and mindfulness and meditation don't fix you or make you a better person.

Instead, they clear away the layers of metaphorical grime that years of negative messages and life's challenges have covered you in, to reveal the beautiful shining lustrous gem at your centre: your true self — which was there all along.

What's draining your power? Name it, and in doing so you'll take away some of its power.

Release it. Write it down on a piece of paper and burn it (under a full moon adds extra power to this!).

And call back your power.

Mind Taming Peace Mantra:

I call back my power now.

Peace Lies Within

Open Your Heart

Within each of us is a heart.

A physical organ, which constantly beats; pumping blood through our body; supplying blood and nutrients to our organs and removing toxins and waste.

But it is so much more than that, essential as that is to stay alive and healthy and well.

The heart is also the centre of our emotional and spiritual wellbeing.

It's the energetic source of love and connection and compassion.

All too easily we can develop emotional armour as we travel through life and we close off our hearts to our own deepest desires, joys and people, in fear of being hurt or abused or judged (again).

But if we travel through life disconnected from our hearts — from this infinite source of love, kindness and understanding — then, well, we're hardly living life at all, are we?

Connecting to the energy of our hearts is a powerful way to tame the mind because when we're connected to the space of our heart, then joy, empathy, humour, courage, understanding, wisdom and love will naturally arise. This space within us doesn't judge or fret or worry. It loves.

That's all it can do because love is our natural state.

So, in this section, I offer you guidance and tools to open your heart. To be kinder to yourself. To soften and allow.

This section includes pieces on self-care because this is a wonderful heart opener AND we need an open heart to allow ourselves the self-care we need. But I'm not talking about mani-pedis or getting your roots done or fun times over Prosecco.

I'm talking about the deep needs we have for meaning and connection, and the practical but often overlooked needs of our bodies.

When we care for ourselves, we feel healthier and whole.

When we care for ourselves, we feel more genuinely compassionate and open.

When we care for ourselves and nurture our inner radiant heart energy, we can live without guilt and pressure. We can embrace all that we have and all that we are and offer our highest self for the good of each other and all living things.

Our planet needs more people with open, loving hearts who live with courage and kindness.

So, open your heart beloved friend for the good of yourself, your friends and family and the whole world.

*

72. Touch the world with your heart

'A beautiful heart, like the rays of the sun, touches many' ~ Chinese Proverb

The heart — just like the brain — emits an electromagnetic field.

According to the HeartMath Institute (HMI), 'The heart generates the largest electromagnetic field in the body.

The electrical field as measured in an electrocardiogram (ECG) is about 60 times greater in amplitude than the brain waves recorded in an electroencephalogram (EEG).'

Their research has shown that the heart's field can be measured several feet away from a person's body.

The heart's electromagnetic field contains certain information or coding — which researchers are trying to understand — that is transmitted within and outside of the body.

The HMI has found that intentionally generated positive emotions can change this information/coding.

So, the thoughts you think and the emotions you feel CHANGE the qualities of the heart's electromagnetic field. Wow! I find this mind-blowing! (And heart-opening!)

So, the Chinese proverb is right — a joy-filled, loving, compassionate heart literally touches all those it comes into contact with.

Mind Taming Peace Mantra:

I choose to radiate loving feelings out to the world.

73. Love the one you're with

... that's you, by the way!

Why are we so rarely encouraged to express love for ourselves?

Can we truly love another if we don't love ourselves first?

And if we're not used to, or even comfortable with, loving ourselves, how do we even begin to go about doing it?

Phew, that's a big topic!

Try this on for size.

How would it feel to know that you are whole and perfect just as you are?

That you have a wellspring of eternal love, bliss and peace within you?

And if you don't believe this, then how about reflecting that it's your social and mental conditioning that distorts this truth and tells you otherwise?

The first step in learning to love yourself is to realise that the story your mind may be telling you about yourself, your past, present and future is just that: a story. A viewpoint made up of preconceptions and judgments all distorted through the lens of your life experience so far; with the messages of our shame-saturated culture added into the mix.

In realising your mind is so often telling you stories, you can then step back, give yourself a little space and begin to notice where and how distortions are entering your viewpoint.

So, next time you find that you're judging yourself harshly — notice it. Stand back from it. Call it out.

And ask yourself, why am I berating myself like this? How can I show myself love instead in this situation?

Open up the door to inviting love into your heart — love for yourself.

Mind Taming Peace Mantra:

I love myself just as I am.

74. Let the light in

We all have an inner critic. That voice inside our heads that gives us a running commentary on how rubbish we are. That little voice that says, 'you shouldn't have said that'; 'why haven't you done this yet?'; 'there's no point'; 'nobody's interested in what you have to say', blah blimmin blah ...

It can get to feel quite dark and chilly within ourselves when our inner critic takes the reigns.

For me, the biggest and most beautiful journey on which my years of yoga, mindfulness and meditation practice have taken me, is to have moved from a place of lack of self-trust, self-belief and self-acceptance to a place of inner strength, trust, resilience and self-appreciation. It's enabled me to open my heart — to myself.

Try this simple visualisation to take a step further in your journey:

> 1. Take your awareness to your solar plexus area (the area above your navel).
>
> 2. Imagine a glimmer of sunlight ... the early morning sun shining here.
>
> 3. Let that glow become brighter and stronger with each breath.
>
> 4. Let this light and warmth rise to and fill your heart ... warm and strong and vibrant light expanding and filling you with each breath.
>
> 5. Let this inner sunrise bring warmth and contentment and love to every part of your being.

Mind Taming Peace Mantra:

I let the light in and shine my unique radiance.

75. Surround yourself with light

Do you pick up on other people's energy? Their moods and vibes?

Maybe, like me, when you're in busy places, you can easily feel overwhelmed by the noise and lights and hub-hub of busy-ness.

Try visualising that you are cocooned and protected by a beautiful crystal-clear white light ... feel it encircling your body.

Sense it shimmering above your skin ... all around you ... feel its strength ... see its beauty.

Let yourself feel safe within this protective light.

Imagine negative or unwanted energies bouncing off this barrier and ricocheting back to their source.

But also know that you can let in whatever energy you want and need to — it's not impenetrable.

This protective light enables you to choose who and what comes into your space.

Know it is always there, lovingly surrounding you.

Mind Taming Peace Mantra:

I surround myself with light.

I am safe and protected.

76. Be kind to yourself

Maybe you're having a crappy day at work, or you're regretting something you said (or didn't say).

Maybe you're trying to improve your health and wellbeing or wanting to change jobs.

Maybe you're on your yoga mat, and your back hurts.

Maybe you're stuck in the perpetual negative spiral of self-critical thoughts.

Maybe you're being unkind to yourself in another way.

There are hundreds of ways we are unkind to ourselves every day. Whether it's through the choices we make in consuming low-nutrition foods and drink; or ignoring our body when we're hurting, or forcing ourselves on when we need to rest, or watching/reading things which aren't good for our peace of mind. Or perhaps merely by listening to our runaway minds telling us we're not good enough or can't do something.

Whatever you're experiencing in your life at this moment, follow this golden rule: **be kind to yourself!**

Find that a challenge?

Well, you can learn to be kind to yourself by tuning in to your wise and loving heart.

Try this:

Move your body to release tensions. Have a bit of a dance, or shake out your arms and legs.

Stretch your arms out to the side and overhead ... breathe deeply to expand your rib cage ... now place the heels of your hands in the small of your back and lift your breastbone ... breathe deeply.

Open up the front of your body ... release restriction from the centre of your chest. Open your heart. With each inhale feel your heart space expanding ... with each exhale release the tension and armoury.

Now sit quietly ... hands resting in your lap ... with a long spine ... once again, gently lift from your breastbone.

Take your awareness to the centre of your chest ... to your heart centre ... ask yourself, 'What do I need to be kind to myself and to show myself love and compassion?' and let your heart answer.

What does it say?

What could you do today to show yourself love? To value yourself? To be kind and compassionate to YOU?

Sit with it. And today, do just one thing that shows you that you love yourself.

And remember...

'*You can search throughout the entire universe for someone who is more deserving of your love and affection than you are yourself, and that person is not to be found anywhere. You yourself, as much as anybody in the entire universe deserve your love and affection.*' ~ Buddha

Mind Taming Peace Mantra:

I listen to the wisdom of my heart.

77. Look after number one

How well do you look after yourself? I mean really pay attention to your needs, especially in relation to the demands other people make on you?

Here's a quick test.

When was the last time you said 'no' to a request from somebody else because you knew that what they were asking didn't feel right or wouldn't be good for you? And you said 'no' without feeling guilty and profusely apologising?

Chances are, you might be struggling to come up with an answer.

Now, I'll say it again! You can't give from an empty well!

By looking after yourself, you will be able to be there for those you love and need you to be your strongest, wisest, most loving and energetic self.

If you keep giving until you're depleted and resentful not only will you make yourself ill, but your tired and frustrated energy will ripple out and will affect all those around you in a negative spiral of bleurgh!

Looked at this way, it's actually selfish *not* to look after yourself isn't it? (Go on, admit it....)

Only when we look after ourselves can we then truly give to others without depleting ourselves. We're no help to anyone if we're burnt-out, knackered and resentful.

Care for yourself first as a selfless act.

If you pay attention to your own needs and feelings, you can begin to work on yourself to release some of the habits and behavioural patterns that lead you to feel stuck in your life.

Learn to check in with yourself throughout the day. Notice how you feel. Where do you feel it in your body? Where do certain emotions or thoughts show up in your body?

Notice, without judgment or analysis. Bring some mindful awareness to yourself. Learn to observe the being that is you.

What do you want from life? What's important to you?

Focus your awareness on what you need, what you want to achieve, and tell yourself that you can and will achieve it. Visualize yourself achieving it and really feel it.

Do the things that bring you joy; whatever fills your cup and helps you feel vibrant, loving, joyful and peaceful.

Whether it's making sure each week you attend your yoga/pilates/swimming/Zumba/art class etc. Or whether it's getting some time on your own. Or spending time with people who light you up: DO IT!

Allow yourself to become you: you do you.

Open your heart to lovingly and courageously allow yourself what it is you truly need.

And if you do that, those around you will pick up on your change in focus, attitude and energy.

Look after yourself, so you can spread good vibes to all who come across your path.

If you work on yourself, you will automatically help those around you because when your sense of wellbeing is healed and strengthened you have so much more compassion, energy and awareness to bring to your interactions with others.

You will be able to act in your life rather than react.

Often, we say we don't have enough time to do the things that nurture us. But is that true or do we make excuses because we've got used to the rush and stress, and are afraid as to what might happen, what we might feel, if we do let go?

Give yourself permission to look into yourself and to look after yourself. Make some time for what you need to nurture and heal the inner you, which may have been ignored for so much of your life.

So, look after yourself. Allow yourself to relax. Allow yourself to let go. Allow yourself to be.

What are you going to do in the next 24 hours to fill up your well?

Mind Taming Peace Mantra:

Self-care is not selfish.

Self-care is essential for my wellbeing.

I give myself the good that I need.

78. Treat your body like a precious object

'Your body is precious. It is our vehicle for awakening. Treat it with care.' ~ Buddha

I love the simplicity of this thought. It brings us back to a grounded reality.

If we follow a spiritual path and/or explore our minds, we may get tempted to dismiss the physical needs of our bodies as we feed our spirit and explore our connection to a higher consciousness.

But the Buddha reminds us that we are physical beings first and foremost. That we inhabit our body for our whole life so if we want to pursue a good life, a spiritual life, we'd better not forget to look after it!

No matter what it looks like, however it may seem to malfunction, your first duty in life is to look after your body.

To listen and to tend to its needs. To eat well. To move, strengthen and stretch it. To listen to its innate intelligence. To read its signals when it warns of stress and overburden. To rest it and let it relax.

If you don't look after your body, then your energy becomes depleted. If you don't eat healthily; if you don't move to the best of your ability; if you dislike or disrespect your body; if you don't show yourself compassion; then how can you connect with others on a meaningful level? How can you empathise with others? How can you love? How can you find happiness and contentment?

The Buddha reminds us that to be born into a human body is an amazing privilege.

We can achieve so much. We can make things. We can create life! We can think. We can contemplate. We can see, touch, smell, hear and taste. We can run, skip and jump.

And so much more besides! And through this body, we can love. And with this body, we can connect to a higher consciousness.

No matter what lumps and bumps you think you have, no matter what ailments, discomforts or disabilities, it is **your** body. Learn to accept it otherwise you will never find peace of mind.

Listen to Buddha – wake up and learn to love your body!

Mind Taming Peace Mantra:

I treat my body with care.

79. Replenish your energy

There are many things you can do to replenish your physical energy — eat well, get enough rest, move regularly.

But don't overlook the subtler aspect of energy: a feeling of inner wellbeing, which is intertwined with the body, mind and soul.

How you feel in yourself and about yourself?

How supported you feel by life in general?

I love to connect to source energy — the energy of the universe. That mysterious life-bringing force and intelligence, which makes the planet spin, and lets plants know when to grow and when to bloom and when to die back.

I experience it as a sparkling, pale shimmering golden light.

An infinite source of love and energy and life. Joyful and playful. Mysterious and wise.

Does this resonate? What does source energy feel like to you?

I invite you now to open up to it and to fill up your well.

Sit or stand.

Bring your hands into praying hands ... palms together ... in front your chest.

Take a moment to connect to your heart ... offering gratitude for all that you have.

And then open your mind and your awareness to the ability to receive what you need.

Raise your hands up in front of your face and continue to raise them over the crown of your head and then open your arms out wide ... open to the heavens above ... raise your face.

Breathe deeply ... breathe and receive all of the energy that you need ... bountiful ... healing ... energising ... nourishing ... rejuvenating.

Breathe and receive all that you need ... be filled up.

Then sweep your arms down to your sides and bring your hands to meet ... as you began ... in praying hands position ... in front of your heart ... and connect to the sense of infinite abundance that is source.

Mind Taming Peace Mantra:

I connect to the infinite energy of the universe

and let myself be filled up with all that I need.

80. Do nothing

When was the last time you did nothing?

Rested? Pondered over a cup of tea? Stared out of the window to watch the clouds? Stood and listened to birdsong? Went for a walk with no aim in particular — just for the love of it? Sat and let your feelings come and go with no judgement?

Recently? Not in ages? Never?

If this isn't something you regularly do, I'm not judging you! I know how difficult it can feel to pack into your days all the activities you need and want to do — let alone finding time to do nothing!

But, this do-nothing-in-particular time is extremely important.

And the fact it is usually overlooked and not allowed in our lives is contributing to the high levels of stress and anxiety as well as fatigue and niggly illnesses in modern life.

Why? Because rest is essential to bring your body and mind back into balance.

It shifts your body out of the stress response, which modern-day life puts it into, and into the relaxation response where your body can rest, digest and heal. Rest balances the nervous system and soothes the mind.

Mind Taming Peace Mantra:

I allow myself to do nothing every now and again

to bring myself back into balance.

81. Let go of compare and contrast

The comparison game. Do you play it?

The constant comparing yourself to others? Not feeling good enough? Feeling frustrated, ashamed, or angry that your life, achievements, appearance don't match up?

Don't feel bad. We all do it and get that sinking feeling of not being good enough in comparison to someone else.

There's something about our culture that promotes comparison.

The glossy magazines, the adverts showing unattainable lifestyles, the sidebars of shame. The carefully curated social media streams designed to illustrate how perfect that person's life is.

Every day we see images and messages that press our 'not good enough' button and leave us feeling anxious, stressed and disappointed.

But it's not good for us to think and feel this way. It erodes our self-esteem.

I'm not immune to it! Confession: social media can press my comparison button!

But then I remember not to compare my life and my rich inner world with the carefully selected images someone else has chosen to show about their life.

Each time we compare ourselves with someone else and find ourselves wanting, we have a choice.

We can let the negative thoughts spiral and beat ourselves up, or we can be mindful of our thoughts.

We can choose to say: 'thank you mind for that thought, but I choose contentment. I am content with what I have now; I am grateful I have the wherewithal and focus to bring into my life what I want and what is good for me.'

I invite you to regularly check in with yourself and how you're feeling with mindful, kind, compassionate, non-judgmental awareness.

And practise contentment and gratitude — it is like building up muscle.

Then when we need it, the sense of contentment and gratitude is stronger than the 'not feeling good enough' response.

Be grateful for your heart beating constantly.

Be grateful for the thousands upon thousands of processes your body performs every second of your life that you're not even aware of. Did you know that your body produces 2.4 million new red blood cells per second, yes, every second? Wow!

Allow yourself to do what brings you joy.

Revel in the contentment the simple pleasures in life can bring — whatever they are for you.

And when comparison strikes, try this:

Stop and look within. Check in with yourself. How does this comparison feel in your body?

You're likely to feel tight somewhere because this feeling is related to shame or envy — and that's not a spacious feeling! You might feel a tightening in the stomach or throat. Learn to know where these feelings manifest in your body. And then...

Breathe out. It's almost impossible to hold onto a tight feeling and thought if we exhale long and smooth. Release the thought, release the feeling of comparison, let it go.

Change your thought. Notice what you're thinking and then choose a new thought.

I say the following to myself when I'm feeling small or fearful:

'I have enough. I am enough. All is flowing as it should.'

Place your hands at your heart and quietly say these phrases to yourself.

I am enough.

I have enough.

I do enough.

I achieve enough.

Let go of comparing.

You are incomparable! You are unique. You are doing the best you can.

And you ARE enough.

Mind Taming Peace Mantra:

I am enough. I have enough.

I am good enough, just as I am.

82. Don't believe the lie that 'you're not good enough'

Throughout our lives, we receive so many messages that tell us we're not good enough.

It could start at school and be reinforced by the continuous rounds of tests and exams. The media and advertising are constantly force-feeding us aspirational messages to encourage us to be discontent with ourselves: 'buy this and you'll be more beautiful / popular / happy / wealthy / successful / better than other people', and so it goes on.

We can become caught in a cycle of trying to please other people and being what we imagine other people think we should be.

We so easily internalise this judging voice and tell ourselves every day the pernicious lie that we're not good enough, often without realising we're doing it.

However, I believe that we are perfect as we are. We have everything we need already inside us. We are full of love, compassion and contentment. We have all the inner resources we need.

We simply need to rediscover this beautiful fact.

It sounds so simple, but I know from experience that it requires self-discipline, awareness, and a willingness and courage to acknowledge the negative thoughts and experiences in our lives and to examine how they have impacted on us, and how they may continue to affect how we behave and think. And then to learn from them and move on.

Here are some practical ways you can reframe your relationship with yourself.

Practise acceptance by learning to notice and be aware, without judgment, of how your body is feeling, the emotions you're feeling and the thoughts going on in your mind.

Extend that acceptance to all parts of yourself and to others.

Witnessing your emotions and thoughts is a vital step in developing a non-judging mind. And if (when!) the inner critic's voice starts judging what you notice, well just witness that too with a gentle awareness.

Also, practise non-violence and be gentle with yourself and commit not to harm yourself by judging and getting angry with your perceived failings.

Practise not wanting what others have. Longing to possess material goods or a lifestyle that someone else appears to have is a sure way to discontentment and feelings of inadequacy.

Practise contentment and be thankful for who you are and what you have in your life. Cultivate a feeling that you lack nothing.

Practise self-study and reflect on who you are, what's important to you and why. Try and read something every day, which is wise and uplifting.

And the next time you notice you're telling yourself that something about you is not good enough, stop and notice ... connect to your heart and smile, because you are perfect just as you are.

Mind Taming Peace Mantra:

I am perfect just as I am.

83. Be courageous

Do you know what? It takes courage to allow yourself to feel and change and grow.

It takes courage to let the feelings in, to allow them to be known to you and to sit and let them pass through.

But so many people in our society are busy numbing out their feelings with busyness, food, alcohol, social media.

What's your oblivion drug of choice? (Confession: when I don't want to think about something I reach for social media.)

To allow yourself to feel, to allow yourself to be tender and open and honest and authentic takes a LOT of strength.
So be brave. Allow yourself to feel.

And you WILL find freedom and happiness; they're there in your heart.

Use the practices in this book; develop a meditation and/or mindfulness practice; connect to yourself and connect to other people; spend time in nature. Do whatever you can to get out of your head and into your heart.

Choose to be courageous and brave in feeling and living honestly and authentically.

As I've said elsewhere in this book, the origins of the word *courage* come from 'cor' the Latin for heart.

The heart is courageous and bold and knows that 'yes', you can, while the mind tends to be timid and restricted and focused on all the reasons you can't.

Yes, you may have been hurt before. Yes, you may feel you have failed before.

But think of these and all the other challenges you've experienced in this life and the feelings they bring as layers — layers of dust, dirt and grime, which are obscuring the real you. The courageous you. The wise and loving you.

Slowly and courageously scrape away the layers of mud to reveal the diamond of bliss, wisdom and peace, which of course, was within you all along.

Be guided by your courageous heart — and embrace all that you are.

Mind Taming Peace Mantra:

I choose to be guided by my courageous heart.

84. Offer yourself love and respect

In our busy, stressful lives, it's easy to forget about ourselves. To forget about our own needs. To forget to offer ourselves the love and respect we may naturally show to others.

When I share this exercise in my yoga classes, it shifts the energy within each person, and it gets extremely positive feedback.

So, rub your hands together vigorously ... activate your heart energy that comes into the palms of your hands ... and then gently pull apart ... can you feel a warmth? A tingling? A resistance?

Imagine you are holding a ball of energy in your hands ... the energy of love and compassion ... the power to offer yourself love and self-respect and healing. Imagine it as a golden ball of light ... a warmth, tingling ... a rosy pink light.

With each breath ... this energy grows a little stronger.

When it feels right ... place your right hand over the centre of your chest and the left hand on top.

As you breathe ... feel you are offering this tender loving energy back to yourself.

Receive love and compassion. You are doing your best. And affirm, silently or out loud: *I am worthy of love, kindness and respect.*

Sit and let yourself receive love, light and healing ... from yourself ... from the heavens above and from your heart.

Choose to feel you are worthy. You are enough.

Mind Taming Peace Mantra:

I am worthy of love, kindness and respect.

85. Be kind

In many ways, we live in uncertain times.

And uncertainty breeds fear. Fear leads to suspicion, which separates us from others.

Connecting to kindness and compassion is essential if we are to keep ourselves free from fear and separation.

So, try this meditation on loving-kindness from the Buddhist tradition:

Sit comfortably ...

Take a few breaths feeling the cool in-breath at your nostrils and the warmer out-breath. Then ground by feeling into the support of the earth beneath you.

Now let your awareness rest at the centre of your chest and silently or quietly repeat these words over and over.

Say it like you mean it (and keep going even if your mind tells you that you don't mean it!)

May I be well
May I be peaceful and at ease
May I be happy

And then expand that intention to send loving kind compassion out into the world.

May all beings be well
May all beings be peaceful and at ease
May all beings be happy

And then rest for a few minutes with your awareness at the centre of your chest — your heart space — and let it be filled with compassion.

You may feel it as warmth or see it as light.

Let compassion fill your heart.

And know that unless we allow compassion into our hearts and show it towards ourselves, we will not be able to truly show it to others.

But when our hearts ARE full of compassion and kindness towards ourselves, we cannot help but feel empathy and compassion for all other beings.

When you're experiencing difficult times, offer yourself love and kindness.

Mind Taming Peace Mantra:

I let compassion fill my heart.

86. Live in harmony

Are your thoughts, words and actions in harmony?

Chances are, there are elements out of kilter in this delicate balance.

Bringing our thoughts, words and deeds into alignment can be a tricky one — especially if we're dealing with a challenging situation or conflict with another person.

But if we don't speak our truth, or we change how we behave to fit in with others' expectations, we will feel misaligned, and this will manifest as stress, anxiety, anger, self-doubt, and frustration.

So how can we find this sense of happiness from balancing our words, thoughts and actions?

Well, I don't have a one-size-fits-all answer!

But I can offer you a starting place: love, kindness and compassion

Practise non-harm: don't harm yourself or others in thought, word or deed.

Start with how you treat yourself and the attitudes you cultivate towards yourself. Be gentle.

So if you are having a bad day or you're feeling down, try acknowledging that this is just how you feel today. You don't need to attach any labels.

This is how you feel in this moment. It doesn't mean you'll feel this way tomorrow. It doesn't define who you are.

You are capable of feeling happy and taking actions which serve your needs.

And today, take action and be kind to yourself, no judgment. So give yourself a hug, and do something to nurture yourself.

As the Buddha said: '*Our own worst enemy cannot harm us as much as our unwise thoughts. No one can help us as much as our own compassionate thoughts*'.

So if a grey cloud is hovering over you today, show yourself compassion. Tell yourself that how you're feeling is fine and all part of being human. Do something that nourishes your body, mind and soul. And just like a grey sky, tomorrow the clouds may lift.

Align yourself with love.

Mind Taming Peace Mantra:

I align my thoughts, words and actions with love.

87. Create a special place

Creating a special place in your home that holds items of significance to you is a soul-nourishing thing to do.

It could be a small table or the corner of a windowsill.

Decorate this space with special items such as pictures of loved ones, images of special places and other unique treasures.

You could make it sacred by adding devotional objects like statues of deities for example. You could place images and items that represent what you'd like to bring into your life.

You might like to bring the elements into it: a crystal for the earth element; a dish of water or a shell; a candle for the fire element; a feather or incense for air. And something that represents source or spirit, such as an image of a deity or something that represents this to you.

Make it an act of devotion to feed your heart and soul by lovingly creating and caring for this space.

Let it be your space to connect.

Sit and meditate in front of it. Place a chair next to it and sit by it while you sip a cuppa. Or just pause next to it for a few moments and allow yourself to slow down, breathe and connect.

Let catching sight of it be a reminder to come out of headspace and busy thoughts, and into the vast and free spaciousness of your heart.

Mind Taming Peace Mantra:

I create and tend to sacred space

to connect to my heart.

88. Feel the love

Whenever we have loved or enjoyed something deeply or felt joy — these feelings become part of us. They can be beautiful memories that are stored in the body as well as in the memory.

If you're going through a tough time in your life, know that all of your experiences of joy, and contentment and love are still there in your heart. Your body doesn't forget those feelings.

Sit quietly and take yourself back to a time when you felt content, happy and safe. Place one hand on top of the other at the centre of your chest and connect to your heart space. Connect to and feel this sense of contentment, happiness and security.

Let this become your inner resource when times are challenging. Your body will respond in turn and feelings of calm and safety will soothe your nervous system.

Connecting to this as an inner resource can provide beautiful solace to keep us going and enabling us to get through dark times.

Remembering that joy stays with us reminds us to savour life and open up to joy and love and enjoy each moment as it comes.

Let these experiences light up your soul and nourish your body with happiness and contentment.

Never underestimate the power of your heart to guide and comfort you and to open you to life, joy, love and possibilities.

Mind Taming Peace Mantra:

I feel the love within my body.

89. Tune your heartstrings

'The heart is a thousand-stringed instrument that can only be tuned with love.' ~ Hafiz

Such a beautiful image!

The heart is central to your physical, emotional and spiritual being.

Of course, a healthy heart organ is essential for life.

But never underestimate the energy of the emotional and spiritual heart in contributing to your wellbeing. The subtle heart is the source of our love and connection, and this source is filled up by love and connection, creating a virtuous circle of healing.

If your heart feels 'out of tune' — heavy, broken, closed up or sore — then ask yourself 'how can I bring more love into my life?'

Offering gratitude for the good you have in your life is a wonderful place to start.

Connecting to someone or something you deeply care for helps you to feel calm, content and at ease and is another way to bring love into your being.

Try this — it only takes a minute:

> 1. Place one hand on top of the other at the centre of your chest and let your awareness rest here ... as if you were breathing in and out through your heart space.

> 2. Now think of something or someone in your life for which you feel deep, sincere gratitude.

3. With your hands still at your heart space and feeling the felt sense of this gratitude imagine each heartbeat sending waves of healing through your whole being.

4. Breathe light and warmth into your heart and let it spread a sense of peace into every cell of your being.

Soothe and nourish your heart with gratitude and love.

Mind Taming Peace Mantra:

I fill my heart with gratitude.

Peace Lies Within

Create Connection

Do you ever get the sense there's something out of kilter?

That something doesn't quite feel right?

A strange but very real sense that something isn't quite connected properly.

What's going on?

Millions of us live in societies and cultures that have, in many ways, lost their sense of connection.

The natural ebbs and flows of energy through the day are ignored. We're expected to be switched on 24/7.

Our consumerist culture tells us to look outside for answers and happiness and to never feel content (otherwise we might stop buying things!).

In a busy-obsessed, productivity-driven culture we've lost alignment with the beautiful lessons and cycles of the seasons, which continuously move through the cycle of birth and growth, maturity, letting go, dying and back to re-birth.

We've lost our connection to meaningful work. Millions of people stay tied to jobs they don't enjoy and can't control. And many people remain stuck in roles that offer no sense of contribution or value to society.

We've out-sourced our health and wellbeing to a medical system that revolves around drugs. Doctors aren't trained to recognise or help with the lifestyle issues which underpin so many conditions and diseases. It's a rare doctor who would inquire into how your mind is affecting your body (and vice versa).

We've lost our connection to each other — often miles away from family, many of us live alone without wider support circles to help us. We're encouraged to see life as a big competition where only the fittest and smartest and loudest wins.

We've lost our connection to spirit, to source. Our soul is yearning to guide us, but we deaden its whispers with social media, food, alcohol, busyness and TV. What's your numbing drug of choice?

No wonder so many countries are experiencing anxiety and depression in epidemic proportions.

There's something deeply out of alignment in the world.

Now, this isn't the book to address the underlying structural issues, but with it, I do hope to help you put a few connections back in place and find your way to a sense of inner peace.

So, with this section, I hope to empower you to bring a sense of connection back into your life through simple actions and perspective shifts, to create a renewed sense of meaning in your life and to strengthen the connections you already have.

It all begins with reconnecting to yourself. To your heart and soul. And then remembering that we are all connected here on this Earth. All of life is one.

*

90. Connect to the power of stillness

Can you remember the last time you felt completely still?

Totally present? Connected to the person or scene in front of you, not analysing, not judging or worrying, just being open to whatever you were experiencing with a grounded sense of stillness?

We can sometimes experience this deep sense of stillness when captivated by a beautifully radiant sunset, or a scene unfolding before us in nature, or when we're enjoying time with friends and loved ones.

But, these moments tend to be few and far between because as soon as we stop and connect to something that transcends our everyday lives — what happens? The mind kicks in and starts its usual running commentary and, bang! We're kicked out of the stillness of that moment, and we're back into analysing, comparing, judging, wishing and resisting.

This reminds me of a short but bitter-sweet line from Eckart Tolle's book *Stillness Speaks*.

'The human condition: lost in thought'.

So true! Hours and days can so easily slip by lost in the whirlpool of the constant rush of thoughts.

However, if you practise and cultivate a sense of stillness within your body and mind you will come to realise that this is your true nature: awake and aware, watching and sensing with an open heart and open mind.

Connect to the power of stillness to calm and rebalance the fight/flight response of your nervous system. You will feel your body soften and relax, and your mind gradually slow down and let go of its constant grip of fruitlessly trying to control everything.

Connect to the power of stillness to slow down, and become more present, and you will begin to notice and appreciate more of the simple pleasures in life to feel more content and peaceful.

Connect to the power of stillness to allow yourself to feel your emotions ebbing and flowing, instead of numbing them with busy-ness, or pushing them away. And in doing so, you will find a sense of gentle compassion arise in your heart, and you begin to be easier on yourself and others and to abide in a sense of calm acceptance and love.

All this comes from cultivating stillness.

You will feel more connected; more compassionate; and more peaceful.

So, how to access this wonderful power of stillness?

Well, you might think it's as simple as just stopping what you're doing and sitting down and closing your eyes in meditation and – ta-dah! – a radiant inner stillness and pure connection to your true nature immediately reveals itself to you.

Well, maybe, but it's not that likely!

Our lives are so busy, and our nervous systems are so over-stimulated that running around all day and then suddenly stopping and expecting to experience delicious, deep peace is pretty much physically impossible.

You need to soothe the body, calm your nervous system and relax first.

A super-quick way to get to this place is to go outside and find yourself a nice old tree. And sit by it. Or if you can't get outside, find a picture or use the power of your imagination. Feel the sense of the tree's deep roots and its amazing stillness. Let that stillness seep into your bones and every cell of your being.

When you cultivate this sense of inner stillness and deep inner peace, you will find that you begin to connect to life more deeply.

You will be more present and open and loving in your relationships.

You will be able to hear the whispers of inner guidance, which will help you to navigate life with a greater feeling of wellbeing and authenticity and integrity, rather than being pulled about by the events and demands of other people.

You will become LESS reactive, judgmental, fretful and stressed and MORE accepting, resilient, present, peaceful, positive and joyful.

Awaken from the slumber of constant rumination and come to your senses; connect to the joy of life by cultivating deep inner peaceful stillness.

Are you ready to let the power of stillness into your life?

Mind Taming Peace Mantra:

I connect to the power of stillness every day

in a way which brings me joy and peace.

91. Check in with yourself

We have so much guidance available to us at every moment — and it comes from within. So ask yourself these questions and let the answers arise without judgement, without pushing some away or grabbing onto others:

How does my body feel, here in this moment? Do I notice any aches or any areas of stiffness? How do my muscles feel? How do my joints feel?

What sensations can I feel within my body? Any sense of warmth or coolness? Any tingling? Any sensations of openness or freedom?

How am I breathing? Deeply? Shallowly? Quickly? Slowly? Roughly? Smoothly?

How is my mind? What thoughts are present? What emotions? Is my mind busy or quiet today? Try to notice without judgement.

What am I perceiving? On a deeper level are there any thoughts coming up that are giving me answers to questions in my life? Any intuitions or insight? Any 'gut feeling'?

How connected do I feel? Does my energy feel scattered or do I feel still and connected, for example, to the earth and sky, to my body, breath, mind and wisdom? To nature? To other people? To a sense of purpose?

Tune into the messages within — let your body, breath and intuition guide you to inner peace.

Mind Taming Peace Mantra:

Every day I choose to stop and listen in

to the messages from my body and mind.

92. Give yourself five minutes

If you're often feeling wired, tired, or wired AND tired at the same time, then it's a sign you need to slow down and give your poor over-stimulated nervous system a break.

Maybe you have a lot of demands on your time, focus and energy from other people, whether it's through work and/or family demands.

Or, maybe it's an internalised feeling of busy that you can't stop; you can't slow down. A feeling of over-stimulation from all the thoughts, feelings, images, memories and plans. (That's the busy that gets me!)

If you're experiencing feelings of anxiety and stress, it's a sign you need rest.

I know I often resist it.

How about you?

We live in a culture that glorifies being busy. Economic productivity is placed above fulfilment and happiness.

The natural ebb and flow of women's energy through the monthly cycle is ignored; the natural ebb and flow of our energy through the seasons of the year is denied.

We're always meant to be switched on, on, ON. Doing, doing, DOING! More, more, MORE!

We internalise it and get addicted to being busy and feel guilty if we're not (yes, I put my hand up to that too! It's an ongoing practice to let that go...).

But if we keep ignoring our need for quiet-time and rest, we end up crashing and burning. Whether it's through a constant cycle of coming down with colds and bugs; digestive issues; or anxiety and stress, or worse.

So, at the risk of repeating myself, I'll say it again: SLOW DOWN AND REST!!

And I don't mean flopping down and zoning out in front of the telly. The constant round of bad news; arguments in soaps; and tension-inducing dramas on the TV will stimulate your nervous system even more.

Ideally, you're looking for something that soothes the nervous system.

Promise yourself at least five minutes a day to do something restful.

Yes, you can.

That's just five minutes out of 1440 minutes each of us has each day.

That's just 300 seconds out of 86,400 each of us has each day.

So, what time can you carve out each day to reset your nervous system and bring yourself into a state of relaxation and self-healing?

Not sure? Try these:

Find a place where you won't be disturbed. Take some calming breaths ... inhale to a count of four and exhale to a count of four.

Stand outside and feel the sun/wind/air/rain on your face. Watch the clouds or the sunlight. Listen to the birds, the wind in the trees, the traffic ... just be with whatever you can hear.

Shake your body – shake your hands, arms, wriggle your shoulders. Shimmy your hips. Shake out your legs and feet.

Get moving. It relieves stress and anxiety and resets the nervous system helping you to feel calmer and more present.

Lie down and practise Crocodile Pose (which is a yoga pose). Lie down on your front, take your feet wide apart and let your heels turn in towards each other. Rest your forehead on the backs of your hands. Withdraw your senses and thoughts from the outside world and to reconnect to yourself. Go inwards to a safe place. Let the earth support you. Let whatever thoughts and feelings are present BE. Don't struggle with them, don't fight them, don't push them away. Breathe and let them be.

Make yourself a cuppa, light a candle and sit and reflect on what you are grateful for in your life. Practising gratitude and contentment is a wonderful balm for the soul.

So, you get the picture. It doesn't have to be fancy-schmancy. Just five minutes a day here and there can help you to realise that feeling stressed and anxious isn't the only option.

Make this non-negotiable, a time for personal space, rest and reflection. Reflect. Just be.

You NEED to give yourself a break.

Jump off the hamster wheel and give yourself a bit of calm space every day, and allow yourself to slow down and connect to the power of peace and stillness.

Be a radical. Rest.

Mind Taming Peace Mantra:

I gift myself at least five minutes every day to rest.

93. Listen to your inner wisdom

I'm sure you're very familiar with your own voice speaking to the world.

And I'm sure you also hear the voice that chatters along inside your head — yes, we all have one. It's a voice that runs its commentary on the day, and yourself. The inner critic that never quite feels satisfied with life.

But have you heard the inner voice of kindness and compassion?

That place of inner knowing. Trust. Wisdom. Guidance.
Call it your soul, your heart, your intuition.

It's so easy for our inner voice of wisdom to be drowned out. Social media, the news, friends, family and colleagues all have their own opinions.

And we inhabit a culture that is suspicious of intuitive feelings and denies their truth.

Or we don't hear it because our monkey mind is jabbering away with random thoughts about nothing in particular.

But that inner voice is there within. Sometimes very quiet, and often shouted down by your hurt ego. But it's still there.

When you slow down and become still, settled, grounded and safe, your inner guidance **will** begin to speak to you.

Have you heard it within you?

A voice that is loving, patient, kind and joyful.

Ready and waiting to be heard, saying, 'It's OK. There's nothing wrong with you. This is life. This is living. It's OK.'

Or maybe it doesn't speak with words.

Your soul whispers may come with feelings, images, voiceless guidance.

It's that intuitive feeling you have when you just know something is right or wrong for you.

Listen.

It will take you to the right path.

Listen.

And step forward with love and trust.

Listen for your inner guide: the wisdom of the quiet voice within you of your heart and soul.

You will be on the right path when you allow your soul to guide you.

The greatest gift you can give yourself is the gift of reawakening your awareness of the wise, loving heart and radiant soul within you which tells you the truth; lovingly guiding you towards the right path.

To hear it, you need to slow down, still the body and quiet the mind.

Try this exercise to listen to the quiet whisperings of your wise and loving heart.

You can listen to a guided version in the resources which accompany this book.

> 1. Sit comfortably in a quiet place. Take some deep soothing breaths to settle. Gradually draw your attention inwards.

> 2. Place your hand on your heart space ... the centre of your chest.

3. If there's a question you need guidance on in your life now, ask your HEART this question ... and listen for an answer.

   a. Imagine an ear at your heart ... listen for the quiet whispers of your inner guidance. It might come as a feeling ... an image ... just allow whatever comes up to come up.

4. Resolve to trust this inner guidance and do something in the next 24 hours to act on the guidance you have received.

What is your heart telling you?

Mind Taming Peace Mantra:

I trust the wisdom of my heart and soul to guide me.

94. Understand your ego

I'm sure you've heard of the ego — that part of us that is associated with self-esteem and our sense of self.

It normally gets a bad rap. Calling someone egotistical is an insult. Doing things to boost your ego will rile other people. Having a big ego is deemed 'A Bad Thing'. In spiritual/new age/personal development circles, displaying any sign of having an ego is a certain sign of not being evolved spiritually, and you're looked down on because of this.

The ego is that mysterious aspect within us, which makes us feel separate from everything else. And this does have serious limitations in terms of creating connection.

But to dismiss this aspect of you and to try to squash and diminish it is actually damaging to your mental and emotional health.

Here's why.

And I'll begin with a question for you.

Who would you be without your sense of self? Without an understanding of your preferences and desires and wishes? Without a sense of your own values?

You'd be no-one. Nothing. Amorphous.

You wouldn't be human.

So please understand that having an ego is not something to be ashamed of — it's part of what it is to be human.

Not knowing who you are and what you want from life and living without purpose is not a road I would wish anyone to take.

We need boundaries and a sense of self to be able to be in healthy relationships with ourselves and others. Otherwise, we just get pushed and pulled around completely at the mercy of other people (and their egos!) and events.

However, (Yes, this is a 'but' here!) ...

While the ego is essential to our sense of an individual self, living and operating in this world, it's not the whole story.

Yes, each of us is an individual separated from other living beings by the physical boundaries of our skin and the individual life experiences we have lived through.

But there's more to each of us than that.

There is a non-physical aspect to you. A spirit, a soul, an essence, a divine spark, universal consciousness — whatever you wish to call it — that exists beyond the ego's sense of separation.

It's in that longing to make meaningful connection. It's in that whisper of inner-knowing and wisdom that arises from deep within. It is expansive and full of wonder. It feels the stardust in each cell of your being and understands that all of life is connected.

And the funny thing is, from my experience at least, it is when we feel most comfortable, accepting and loving towards our individual self (the ego) with all our quirks and weirdness and imperfections, that this sense of deep connection to all-that-is can be felt.

Allow yourself to embrace all that you are and all that you have experienced — the joys and the challenges. Allow yourself to find peace with your mind — no matter how noisy, critical and downright annoying it is. And you may just find yourself transcending the boundaries of your small sense of self to know, deep in your bones and every fibre of your being, that there is more to life than your little self.

That you're not separated from life.

That you exist in a delicate web of energy and awareness and life, which connects us all.

Allow yourself to have your ego and sense of self and accept this.

And be OK with it. Let go of the struggle. You're you. You're unique.

And in allowing this let in the possibility that you're also deeply connected to the whole pulse of life: timeless and beyond boundaries and radiantly divine.

Mind Taming Peace Mantra:

I am me, and I am we, and we are all connected.

95. Feel connected

It's easy, in this crazy, busy world, to feel that we are ineffectual; that our actions and words don't change anything. Or the opposite — to want to shrink away and hide from an over-stimulating, unkind world.

But we are all noticed.

We are all of us noticed by everyone with whom we interact, even if in tiny, subtle, unconscious ways.

Even if you sit in a room, or in a group and don't speak, you are affecting the energy in that place. The people you are with will, to a lesser or greater extent, pick up on how you are feeling and this, in turn, will affect them.

This could be through body language or subtler 'invisible' energies such as picking up 'bad vibes' from someone who you feel is in a bad mood but hasn't said a word about it.

You will have influenced hundreds and thousands of people you've never actually 'met', but your energies crossed as you passed on the street or sat on a train. And of course, you're constantly affecting the people you see every day, whether that's family, friends or colleagues.

How we are when we go out into the world has an effect like ripples on a pond.

A smile at a stranger could change their mood and alter how they feel in that moment, which could in turn, transform how they relate to the people they come across that day.

Saying a heartfelt 'thank you' to a friend or a colleague when they've helped you out could deepen your relationship.

Cultivating a feeling of gratitude could transform your life and alter the way you interact with everyone you meet, and could inspire others to live with a positive attitude.

We are all connected, whether we realise this or not.

And remember, you can choose the quality of the energy you radiate. Loving or fearful? Happy or grumpy? Content or envious?

No matter what is happening in your life, you can decide how to deal with it and in turn, this will determine the effect you have on all those around you.

Be aware your energy leads the way. And never think you're invisible!

Mind Taming Peace Mantra:

I am connected to all that is.

96. Rise up

Kept low by our fears and worries of lack and shame we live a half-life of comparison and envy.

Fed lies by those who profit from us, not living our true potential we skulk and sulk and lash out at others.

But in my bones and my mind's eye, I have felt and seen a different way.

And this I now know:

When we shake off the shackles of our conditioning.

When we refuse to compare and compete.

When we rise as communities and citizens and refuse to be passive consumers.

When we see what unites us and leave behind what we're told separates us.

When we call out the lies of vested interests and pull the scales from our eyes.

When we choose love and connection over fear and division.

When we root down to Mother Earth and appreciate Her abundance.

When we look up to the moon and sun and stars and breathe the infinite wonder of the universe.

When we see the deep beauty in a flower.

When we see the radiant life in another's eyes.

When we connect to our hearts and immerse ourselves in the infinite peace and strength and wisdom that reside there.

Then we realise the true nature of ourselves and the universe: LOVE.

And when we immerse ourselves in this truth, fear falls away — and we rise.

And when we rise, awakened to our power and our connection to all that is, and live and act from a place of powerful, peaceful, presence, we can embrace life and all its challenges with a profound and soulful YES!

Mind Taming Peace Mantra:

I rise in love.

97. Live your life in alignment

Does something seem out of alignment in your life?

Maybe you know what it is. Perhaps you can't quite put your finger on it, but it's a niggling sense that something needs to change.

Perhaps your body, mind and soul are out of alignment with each other.

In the introduction to this section, I outlined some of the ways that our society has become misaligned.

On an individual level, there are many ways that we can be living out of alignment:

- Eating unhealthy food.
- Lack of sleep.
- Working in a role that doesn't align with our principles and values.
- Too much sitting — not enough movement.
- No downtime.
- As a woman, being unaware of the natural fluctuations of energy throughout her monthly cycle.

That's just a few of the myriad of ways — can you think of more?

Well, it's time to realign.

I believe we are the creators of our own reality.

Through the thoughts you CHOOSE to think, to the actions you CHOOSE to take, it IS possible to smooth out the kinks!

And when one person chooses a better way, that energy flows out throughout their life and touches others.

It's about listening in and connecting — to yourself.

It's certainly not about aligning yourself to external pressures and messages about what you ought to do/be/look like/possess.

It's about re-learning to trust yourself.

A re-membering. Putting yourself back together after being pulled apart by external forces that only want to reshape you into a model, docile consumer who doesn't think for themselves.

Take control of your life.

Look at these three areas within your life and make a conscious decision to reconnect: to realign. These can be tiny little steps — they soon build. And you'll look back and see how far you've come!

Here are some simple suggestions.

1. Learn to listen to your body's needs for nourishment, movement, rest and relaxation.
This is a huge topic. With so much 'food' in supermarkets containing very little nourishment; with our forced sedentary lifestyles often chained to a desk; never being able to switch off so our bodies don't get the rest and relaxation they need to maintain equilibrium. It's no wonder there's so much stress and stress-related illnesses in our society.

Tips: do some simple stretches when you get up in the morning. Get up from your desk and go for a walk at lunchtime. Swap one cup of coffee a day for herbal tea or water.

2. Learn to listen to the messages coming from your mind and emotions.
If you often feel angry, don't just try to deaden it or numb it. Feel it and ask the anger what message it has for you.

What positive action can you take to transmute the energy of anger into something proactive? Approach moods and emotions as messengers. Don't push them down or bottle them up — they'll explode in your face otherwise!

Tips: next time you feel a powerful emotion such as anger, fear, doubt — simply notice it. With mindful compassion and curiosity breathe with it and see how it feels in your body. And ask it what action you need to take so you can positively use the energy, rather than letting it eat you up.

3. Learn to listen to your soul and spirit and intuition.
Those whispers of inner guidance, which deep down you know are right, even if your mind gets worried and tries to convince you they are wrong. Connect to your soul, your heart, your spirit. That place within you full of wisdom, peace and joy.

Tips: At least once this week give yourself five or ten minutes to sit still, breathe. Let body and mind settle. Place your hand on your heart and ask yourself, 'what do I need to know?' Without expectation or judgment let your inner guidance whisper to you.

Mind Taming Peace Mantra:

I live my life in alignment

with the needs of my body, mind and soul.

98. Watch the ripples

We are all connected. Whatever we do or say will affect others whether we realise it or not.

The decisions you take and actions you begin today will ripple throughout your life and affect the lives of others.

Cultivate awareness and notice the true intentions behind your words and actions. Be aware that your words and actions ripple through your connections and throughout your life.

Surely it's better to try to ensure that the ripples emanate from a place that is positive rather than negative?

Take a deep breath, which prevents an angry reaction.
Pick up the phone to reconnect with a friend.

Share a difficult experience you've overcome to support someone else going through a bad time.

Who knows what effect they might have?

Consciously try to put out positive energy into the world yet don't become attached to what this might lead to.

Run your decisions past an internal filter and ask yourself where they are coming from: fear and contraction, or hope, love and expansion?

And if you discover a choice that has been based on fear, well, don't beat yourself up. Be kind to yourself. The first step in changing this is knowing your habits.

With an open heart and courageous love and kindness, resolve to choose love as the basis for your decisions, actions and words.

Let the waves flow away from you and touch who they need to.

So, go on, choose to throw a pebble in the waters of your life; a pebble that has the words 'calm', 'love', or 'health' written on it.

And create ripples that have a positive effect on yourself and the world.

Mind Taming Peace Mantra:

I choose to radiate love out into the world.

99. Ponder on inner power

What does 'power' mean to you?

You may have mixed feelings.

The concept of power has become messed up in our culture. Power is usually equated with power OVER someone or something else. It's often seen as destructive; manipulative.

But true power in a personal context is about our personal power; our inner resilience and determination and willpower.

The power to harness your mind to focus and to shape your destiny.

An inner fire, which is the flame that transforms, burning away the habits and foggy thinking that cloud your true nature.

Connect to this inner power through visualisation.

Imagine a fire burning in your belly, or feel the rays of the mighty sun in your solar plexus area, sending light and warmth out in all directions.

Form this hand mudra (gesture) — **The Gesture of Fire**:

> 1. Place your left hand, palm face up in front of your solar plexus (the area just above your navel). Then form a thumbs up gesture with your right hand and place this hand on the left palm with the back of this hand facing away from you.

> 2. Allow feelings of inner strength and resilience to grow and glow within you.

> 3. Offer any limiting beliefs or behaviours or emotions to the fire of transformation.

Embrace your inner fire and your inner power and live your life with a fire in your belly; warmth in your heart; and a bright, clear mind.

You have the power to determine how you act or react or interact with whatever is going on in your life and how you deal with others.

Choose not to be a victim of circumstance or a martyr to the perceived failings or irritations of others.

In realising and embodying this — therein lies your true power.

Mind Taming Peace Mantra:

I embrace my inner fire as a force for good.

100. Be a peaceful warrior

You are working for peace. Did you know that?!

Each of us who is on the path of self-growth and healing is a peace worker.

When we commit to understanding ourselves, releasing our limiting beliefs and showing up in this world bravely and wisely, we are working to spread peace, acceptance and compassion in our lives and our communities.

By showing up, by setting your intention to feel calmer, stronger or more at ease with yourself, you are spreading peace in this world.

By choosing to breathe and let go.

By choosing to notice the thoughts and let them be.

By choosing to do something that makes you feel better about yourself.

By resolving to change your perspective from frustration to acceptance.

With these seemingly small decisions, you will send out a more peaceful energy, which spreads through your life and into the lives of others.

Be a light filled divine warrior of peace and love, empathy and understanding, loving action and support.

Claim your power.

Shine your light.

Let go of the limiting beliefs that tell you that you can't, or that you're not good enough.

Shake off the mind-forged manacles, which keep you chained to thoughts, behaviours and things that no longer serve you.

Radiate your unique soul-essence out into this world.

Mind Taming Peace Mantra:

I choose to spread peace in this world.

101. Be the change

What annoys you about other people? What makes you angry or frustrated? What acts that you see perpetrated against others, sadden you?

What do you think needs to change in the world to make it a better place?

Perhaps you think there should be more compassion, more honesty, less game-playing, less division. Maybe you think individuals need to take more responsibility for their health and their lives, or maybe you think more support should be provided for people who are disadvantaged.

We all have our own opinions about our friends, family and colleagues, workplaces and the society we live in.

This can lead us to go through life passively judging and complaining. (And I'm not judging anyone by saying that — I know I have done that myself!)

It's not surprising we often feel powerless. We're treated as passive consumers by the blitz of marketing we're forced to navigate through every day of our lives. Our trust in politicians and public bodies has been eroded by numerous scandals and stories of collusion and corruption.

It all adds up to feeling powerless to do anything about it.

But if we stop and look at our own lives and how we live, and take affirmative steps to improve ourselves, then perhaps we can reverse this tide of powerlessness and claim back some strength and control.

What change do you want to see?

Identify what you'd like to change in your world, or in wider society, and take a few moments to see how you can embody that.

And now identify what actions you can take to change your world. As Gandhi said, '*Be the change you want to see in the world*'.

Are you fed-up with lies? Then tell the truth.

Does seeing fear in others sadden you? Then strive to be courageous in what you do and say.

Do you want to see peace? Stop fighting against yourself. Accept yourself as you are and stop the struggle within.

Are you sick of game-playing and politics at work? Then don't get caught up in politicking yourself. Don't indulge in gossip. Be honest and straightforward. I know this can be tough if you're going against the prevailing workplace culture, but for your peace of mind and sense of self-worth, choose to act in a way that is authentic to your higher self.

Do you want to see an end to scandal and dishonesty in public life? Then be truthful and upstanding in your life. Maybe see how you can contribute to the public good and take action. Volunteer with a local organisation or give money/time/goods to charity.

And if you feel powerless to change anything, then reflect on these words from the Dalai Lama: '*If you think you are too small to make a difference, try sleeping with a mosquito*'.

Know that you can make a difference. You can change your own world for a start.

If we start to be that change we want to see, it will cause a ripple effect.

Our family, friends and colleagues will feel it — consciously or unconsciously. We may come across resistance from those around us as we change and grow. But actually, they may be inspired to make small or large changes themselves and in turn, connect with their family, colleagues and friends.

And so it goes on.

Learn to stand in your power, your beauty, your compassion and your ability to change the world for the better.

And play your part in changing this world for good.

Mind Taming Peace Mantra:

I embody the change I want to see in the world.

102. Awaken to your true nature

Everything in our culture encourages us to look outside ourselves for answers and validation.

It starts at school, and as we grow up and throughout adulthood we're conditioned to look to 'experts' to tell us what's going on inside ourselves; we're told to buy, buy, buy, all sorts of stuff to make ourselves feel happy; we're taught that material possessions and career advancement are indicators of our worth.

No wonder so many of us feel disconnected and discombobulated and confused. We're inhabiting a twilight zone of disconnection. As a human race, we have created this dream (or nightmare) that we are all in competition to prove our worth to each other.

We're self-medicating with TV, busy-ness, food, drink, social media and drugs to numb out the insistent feeling that there has to be another way.

And there is.

Turn away from competition. Turn away from wanting more. And look inside yourself for the answers and contentment.

Follow these wise words:

'*Who looks outside dreams. Who looks inside awakens*' ~ Carl Jung

Awaken to the inner wisdom of your body/mind.

Your body is continually giving you feedback on how you feel.

The tension in your jaw and throat, for example, suggesting you're not speaking your truth. The digestive woes, indicating there's something about your life that you can't stomach. The lower back, hips and knee niggles that point to an absence of flow in life and of being ungrounded.

Slow down, look within and hear the whispers.

I'm not saying it's easy. When we look within we may find all sorts of emotions and feelings we've been suppressing for years. Allowing yourself to feel them is part of the process.

If it all feels too difficult, then simply look within and ask what simple pleasures bring you joy.

And gift yourself moments of joy every day to feed your soul.

Look within and wake up to your true human nature and potential: wise, infinite, loving.

It's always there.

It's like the sky.

The sky is always there above us — it appears to change yet it is constant. It undeniably exists, but if we try to reach out and touch it or locate it we find it's impossible to do so.

It just is.

In this way, our true nature is like the sky.

It is always there within us. It appears to change yet it is constant.

We try to find it — often by looking outside ourselves for validation or confirmation, or looking for external things to bolster our sense of who we are.

Instead let yourself be open to what mystics and spiritual teachers have experienced and taught for centuries: we are unbound, pure awareness; sparks of divine light and love and joy incarnated into human beings.

This is your true nature.

You don't need to go looking for it.

It's there and within you all along.

It's perhaps that you've forgotten. Your fretful mind tells you stories about how you're not good enough somehow, or life experience has battered you and taught you to feel insignificant.

Let these stories go.

Stop searching.

You were there all along.

Radiant and loving.

Strong and grounded.

Free and vast.

Joyful.

Mind Taming Peace Mantra:

I look within and awaken to my true nature.

103. Align your heart to heaven and earth

Practise this beautiful technique to connect within and to all that is.

> 1. Sit quietly and comfortably. Close your eyes. Let your breath settle.
>
> 2. Take a few breaths to connect to the earth beneath you: strong and solid and safe and still.
>
> 3. Breathe this strength and stillness up through the base of your spine to your heart ... pause ... then breathe out through the top of your head.
>
> 4. Take a few breaths to connect to the heavens above; spacious ... vast ... limitless and free.
>
> 5. Breathe this spacious freedom in through the crown of your head to your heart, pause ... then breathe out down through your body and out through the base of your spine to the earth.
>
> 6. Repeat this breathing awareness for a few minutes ... aligning to the earth below ... the heavens above ... drawing their energies into your heart.
>
> 7. To finish, rest with your awareness within your heart space ... aligned with and connected to all the support around you.

That's it. So simple and so grounding and connecting.

Mind Taming Peace Mantra:

I connect to my heart, to the heavens and the earth.

104. Tune into your heart

Which rules within you? Your head or your heart?

It's a tricky one.

Should you make choices based on logic, analysis and perceived knowledge, or make them based on inner guidance, which often arises as a strong feeling in the body, and may defy logic?

I always used to live in my head, but it was a fretful space to occupy, so now I make it my daily spiritual practice to tune into my heart.

Because, '*Your heart knows the way. Run in that direction*' ~ Rumi

These words are the essence of why I teach and share what I do!

When you settle the body and quieten your mind you will find that you begin to hear a gentle voice whispering to you — the voice of inner wisdom.

Whether you feel it's your heart, your soul, your intuition or the voice of God/dess talking to you — we all have access to this inner guidance.

Trouble is, our fretful analytical mind is so loud it too often drowns out the quiet, wise whisperings of our soul.

And add to that a culture, which denigrates listening to your heart and tells you to listen to your head over your heart, says being emotional is weak, and teaches you to cut off from your intuition; that quiet voice within which somehow just seems to know.

Let me be clear. This inner guidance is not the analysing logical mind that feels it has to be right and sure before making a decision, and then frets over the outcome.

This inner guidance does not use words like 'should' or 'shouldn't'.

This inner guidance doesn't make us feel guilty for following our own wishes or doing something that lights us up.

This inner guidance leads us to joy, to growth, to healing. It's an intuitive, visceral feeling in the body, which says 'yes, this is right'.

It shows us the way.

How many times have you over-ridden an intuitive instinct about something or someone and let your fretful mind over-rule it, only to realise, all too late, that your inner guidance was right all along?

Time to stop that!

Slow down. Breathe. Bring your nervous system back into balance. Rest. Ground.

And prepare to listen out for the wise whispers of your heart and soul.

The mind tends to inhabit a place of doubt, judgment and analysis.

The complex, wonderful, infuriating mind won't get it. It might even tell you that this deep knowing is wrong or untrustworthy or flighty or a figment of your imagination.

But once you've heard the wisdom of your soul you'll remember how it feels and how it speaks to you. And a part of you will never forget.

Because your heart speaks with love. Your heart contains no judgement but offers acceptance. Your heart energy is never fearful it is trusting and confident.

'Remember, your heart loves you'.

I found those words coming out of my mouth at the end of teaching one of my yoga classes.

It felt slightly woo-woo as I said it, but I'm a firm believer in letting through any messages that come to me when I'm teaching. It means at least one person in the room needs to hear it.

Maybe you need to hear this?

Inside you, deep in your heart, is the deepest wellspring of love.

It has your best interests at heart. It loves you more than you can ever know. But too often our fearful mind gets in the way and we judge ourselves and beat ourselves up.

Listen to your heart. That quiet, kind whisper of tenderness and kindness. And be kind to yourself.

So, breathe out deeply and fully. Let go. Let your awareness drop to the rise and fall of your breath at your chest and abdomen.

Drop into awareness of your heart.

In your heart, you will find balance. You will find the answer you are seeking.

Mind Taming Peace Mantra:

My heart knows the way,

and I trust my heart to guide me.

105. Connect to the cycles of life

Since the beginning of 2016, I've been living differently.

I've been recognising and honouring the cyclic nature of life, and of life as a woman. I've been attentive to the seasons as they change. I've been marking the old Celtic festivals of the summer and winter solstices, the spring and autumn Equinoxes and Imbolc in early February, Beltane at the end of April/beginning of May, Lammas at the end of July/start of August and Samhain at the end of October.

I've been watching the cycles of the moon phases.

And I've been honouring the cyclic nature of being a woman: the monthly cycle.

And alongside this, I've been watching and noticing the ebb and flow of my energy and how it interacts with these cycles.

Not forgetting that cycle that is within us each and every moment: the constant cycle of the inhale ... exhale ... inhale ... exhale ...

And what has this brought me?

It's brought me home.

It's brought me into touch with the earth and the cycle of the moon, sun and seasons. It's brought me into touch with my needs and has connected me to my inner landscape. It's brought me home to my sensitive nature. It's taught me to see how I can tune into the subtle energies of the shift in light and energy in nature, and the shifts of my energy and focus as they change throughout each month.

It's a reclaiming. A tuning in. A recalibration.

A reclaiming of my inner power and wisdom; to genuinely know what I need; to allow myself and give myself to nurture, and honour my needs.

I encourage you, if you don't already, to get in touch with the cyclic nature of life.

Seasonal Energy

So, let's look a little deeper, beginning with the energy of the seasons.

Spring
New life springs forth! As daffodils bloom and the first shoots on trees bud, we can tap into this rising energy ourselves and let the seeds of ideas we nurtured over winter now begin to grow.

Ask yourself, what is rising within me? What is ready to burst forth?

Summer
Summer is the height of the growing season. All is on-show. Energy is high. Tap into abundance and light and life. Choose to do things that bring you joy.

And in late summer — take stock of your own personal harvest. What flourished this year? Be grateful. Give yourself credit for what you've achieved. Reflect on what could have gone better and what might you do differently next year.

Autumn
The energy of autumn is all about letting go. As the trees let go of their leaves, look within and ask yourself, 'what am I ready to let go of?' What's falling away? It could be material possessions we no longer need. It could be habits; ways of being; even people.

Tune into autumn and let go of what you no longer need.

Winter

Winter is the death of the old. The trees are bare. The air is cold. The ground is hard. All seems barren.

But look deeper and realise that the energies have merely gone inwards — hibernating, conserving, ready to flourish when the time is right, in spring.

And we can do the same. Snuggle up with a blanket and book. Allow quiet-time. Conserve our energy. Meditate. Look within. Identify what new seeds we wish to nurture ready to grow next spring …

… and so the cycle continues.

The cycle of the moon

And these cycles can also be seen each month — in the phases of the moon.

The waxing moon is spring-like in energy, growing, expansive.

The full moon is like summer, bright and abundant.

The waning moon has autumn-like energies, a falling away and letting go.

And the dark moon/new moon is winter: a time of inner reflection, ready for the cycle to continue.

The monthly female cycle

And all of this is also reflected in the phases of a woman's menstrual cycle (and if you don't menstruate you can still follow these changing energies by tapping into the phases of the moon. They're all interconnected).

Days 7-14 (pre-ovulation) are spring-like when energy rises.

Days 14-21 (ovulation) are summer, where we are fertile, abundant, full of life.

Days 21-28 or whenever bleeding starts (pre-menstruum) are autumnal where we are getting ready to let go and clear out (and don't suffer fools gladly!).

Days 1-7 (menstruation) are like winter: the death of the old as we bleed and release. And then spring comes around again.

(Male readers take note: be aware of these phases to support the women in your life!)

*

Living in harmony with the cyclic nature of life is a way of coming into union with life.

Tuning into the seasonal shifts of nature is beautiful. We are, after all, part of nature and interdependent with our earth.

Realising, as a woman, that you are shifting through the seasons every month is deeply empowering.

Knowing that all of life is cyclic, liberates us because we truly realise what goes around comes around.

Mind Taming Peace Mantra:

All is change. This too must pass.

106. Connect to nature

'With an eye made quiet by the power of harmony, and the deep power of joy, we see into the life of things.' ~ William Wordsworth

Have you ever experienced that sense of deep connection?

When you feel grounded and present and still, and you can feel the web of life holding you and all living beings in its care?

Gentle, soulful, flowing yoga and meditation, or walking in woodland, or staring out to sea can take me to that place that Wordsworth is talking about.

I've had a few memorable experiences of this over the years.

The first time I felt that deep connection was on a yoga retreat.

We were sent outside to go and gaze at a flower or a tree.

I stood looking at the leaves of a tree.

Suddenly and perceptibly I felt and knew that they were looking back at me.

It was a surprise, yet felt so natural.

We are surrounded by life.

We are interconnected within a web of life.

When we slow down, calm our nervous system and quieten the monkey mind, we realise that all life is connected.

It's a beautiful and deeply soul-nourishing experience.

When your head is full, and your heart is heavy, and you need a reminder that there is something else beyond your worries try this:

Look up into the vast sky and watch the clouds drift by and let your worries drift away with them.

Let your mind be as open and vast as the sky.

Let in the light of perspective.

Gaze at a flower. Such perfection, such beauty, such simplicity. A flower doing all it knows: blooming. Without comparison, without fear it simply unfurls and glows.

In the words of Vincent Van Gough:

'If you truly love Nature, you will find beauty everywhere'

We don't have to look far to see examples of beauty and perfection in nature. But remember, you too are a child of nature. Created by the same light from the sun, and nourishment from the earth, and life from the air around us.

Gift your mindful attention to the simple beauty around you, and nature will gift you with soul food in return.

You too are the perfection of nature embodied in human form.

Hold yourself in a space of love and embrace your natural perfection.

You are a being of light.

All life on this miraculous planet comes from stars exploding billions of years ago.

Stardust fills every cell of your being.

Our sun radiates life, and you receive it every moment of your life.

You are ancient, you are amazing, you are wise.

You are a celestial being.

You are one with the earth.

Remember this when you feel small, confused, overwhelmed and tired.

Feel the earth beneath your feet … and seek the light.

Connect to the light.

Feel the light.

Be the light.

Beloved star child of nature that you are.

Mind Taming Peace Mantra:

I am part of the web of life.

107. Look within

Slow down.

Close your eyes.

Breathe deeply.

Let the white noise of your mind fade away.

Look within.

Listen.

Drop down into the cave of your heart.

Can you feel a tender sweetness there? A place of peace and grace and love?

Can you feel your wise and loving heart? Your soul space?

A place of connection to all that is. To the earth; to the stars; to the whole of life; to the cosmos.

A place beyond time. An ancient knowing. Where past, present and future merge into one.

Expansive. Free.

This is your true self.

Trust in this place. Come back to this space as often as you can.

And welcome yourself home.

Mind Taming Peace Mantra:

I come home to my soul space every day.

108. Reawaken your radiant soul

I believe, no ... I KNOW, that within me, within you and within all of us is a sacred place. A place of deep knowing and wisdom. Timeless. Expansive. Free. Radiant.

It's your soul.

A place of intuitive understanding and deepest peace.

An inner voice, which whispers, whose subtle guidance is all too often drowned out by the loud, fretful, analytical mind.

The voice of your inner wisdom is wise and loving and doesn't shout or fret or judge. Its message is truth and love and may come to you in words, or images or feelings.

Open your inner ears and eyes.

Within you is radiance.

A multi-faceted precious jewel.

Sparkling. Complex. Ancient.

The jewel within your heart.

The seat of the soul.

Its light cannot be diminished.

And yet, we tell ourselves we are small and unworthy, not good enough, imperfect.

We dim our light and hide for fear of being seen.

Life brings layers of hurt, pain, fear and resentment that shrouds the inner jewel and dims its light.

But that luminescence is still there.

Breathe. Move. Release. Be still.

Sink down in the cave of your heart, and you will feel something shimmering.

An unvanquishable energy pulsating and burning and shining, no matter what tries to cover it.

Spend time in the cave of your heart.

Linger with this burgeoning feeling as it begins to peel away the layers covering that inner jewel.

Let the light shine.

Don't shield your eyes from its awe-inspiring luminosity.

This is your sacred soul revealing itself to you.

Let it glow. Let it dazzle. Let it expand.

Feel the joyful peace filling your heart — the natural pure loving joy of being alive.

Revel in this feeling.

Reveal and embrace and live from this place: your radiant soul.

Mind Taming Peace Mantra:

I let my radiant soul shine.

And finally ...

A prayer for inner peace

If you've ever seen or used a set of mala beads, you will know that while there are 108 beads used to meditate with, there is also a 109th bead: the Guru bead.

The Guru bead signifies the end of one cycle of mantra or prayer repetition. It is never counted and provides a moment to pause and reflect.

In this spirit, I offer you the following bead of guidance and inspiration, and an opportunity to pause and reflect before you begin the next cycle within your day.

They're words that came to me, fully formed, as I sat with the late-summer sun shining down on me in the Chalice Well Gardens in Glastonbury in August 2017.

A prayer for inner peace.

It's simple and short. Take some time to linger with it.

Breathe deeply and feel it. Let it into every cell of your being. Let it into your soul.

I hope it resonates with you.

I breathe in divine light ~ universal energy:
Through the crown of my head ... and the soles of my feet.
I feel it flowing down through me ...
rising up ... filling my heart.
Please wash away my doubts and fears.
Please fill me with strength and wisdom
and joy and peace...
... that I may shine my light in this world.

Peace Lies Within

Thank you

And so we come to the end of this book.

I sincerely hope you have found inspiration and guidance within these pages to empower you to tame your mind and connect to inner peace.

My dearest wish for you is to connect and come home to the deep love and wisdom, which is in your heart and soul.

I have tried to share so many ways you can do this within this book. But I know there are many more. Look within and ask yourself and let your soul guide you back to wholeness.

Please know and trust that the little shifts and changes you make in your thoughts and words and actions DO make a difference.

Keep going; keep connecting; keep spreading the peace, which lies within you, out into this world.

Thank you for being a peace-seeker and peace-bringer. Thank you for committing to nurturing that inner peace every day, so you can take your place within the growing community of human beings currently living on this earth who are dedicated to choosing peace over conflict and love over fear.

May the peace that lies within you light up the world.

With so much love,
Stella x

P.S. If you loved this book then please spread the *Peace Lies Within* message. You could post a short review on Amazon; share about it on social media; or tell your friends about it. Thank you!

What Next?

Even more inner peace

Float on over to my website to receive free recordings of some of the meditations and practices from the book: livingyogawithstella.com/peace-lies-within-resources

Body scan #6
Breath comforter #31
Melt the emotional ice meditation #46
Acceptance meditation #58
Inner Smile meditation #62
Cord Cutting meditation #63
Solar relaxation #66
Listen to your inner wisdom meditation #93

Stay connected

Sign-up for Soul Wisdom Mail

Bring some peace to your email inbox by signing up for *Soul Wisdom Mail* at: stellatomlinson.com

Keep in contact

Website: stellatomlinson.com

Facebook: facebook.com/stellatomlinson

Instagram: @stellasoulwisdom

Spread some peace across social media: share about this book, or post your pictures of or inspiration from this book using the hashtag #peacelieswithinbook

I Recommend

Here is a small selection of resources I personally recommend to support you in your journey to connect to inner peace.

Books

Barrington, Chris and Mansukh Patel *Points of Balance* (Dru Publications)

Collard, Patrizia *Journey Into Mindfulness* (Bounty Books)

Elliot, Rose *Every Breath You Take* (Watkins Publishing)

Hall, Jean *Breathe* (Quadrille)

Kempton, Sally *Meditation for the Love of It* (Sounds True)

Patel, Mansukh et al *The Dance Between Joy and Pain* (Dru Publications)

The Happy Buddha *Mindfulness and Compassion* (Leaping Hare Press)

Thompson, Claire *Mindfulness and The Natural World* (Leaping Hare Press)

Yoga and meditation

There are many styles and approaches to yoga and meditation. I (mainly) teach and practice Dru Yoga and Meditation – it really is like no other style I've experienced!

It combines movement (including unique Energy Block Release sequences) with conscious breathing, deep relaxation, mudra (hand gestures), meditation, visualisations and affirmations to bring about deep transformation and relieve the pressures of modern living.

Find out more at **druyoga.com** that includes details of their yoga, meditation, health and wisdom events; retreats; training courses; and publications and a 'Find a Teacher' search. They also have an online studio with a plethora of yoga, relaxation and meditation practices, with more added each month.

Mala beads

Mala beads can be used as an aid in meditation – and worn as a piece of sacred jewellery to connect you to a particular intention or energy.

I recommend Chant Malas: they're beautifully designed, high quality, vegan/ethically-sourced, consciously-crafted mala beads made by Helen, here in the UK, with your meditation practice in mind to honour your mantra practice and feed your wild soul.

Visit: **chantmalas.co.uk**

I am proud to be part of the 'Chant Sisterhood' and as such I would love to share with you my 15% discount code when you register to receive the resources which accompany this book: **livingyogawithstella.com/peace-lies-within-resources**

Apps

I use the free **Insight Timer** app to support my meditation practice. Use the timer or listen to one of the many guided meditations or music pieces. Available for Android and iPhone.

Acknowledgements

A huge thank you to every person who has come to one of my yoga and meditation classes or events since I began teaching in 2012. I couldn't do what I do without you! Thank you for being open to helping yourself and in doing so, increasing the love and compassion on this planet.

I humbly bow in gratitude to the lineage of teachers and practitioners of yoga and meditation reaching back thousands of years. I feel your support behind me and I honour your wisdom.

Thank you to my first yoga teacher, Mary Madhavi, who awakened a love of yoga within me and started me on this journey. Thank you to Sue Homer who introduced me to Dru Yoga at just the right time in my life! Thank you to my Dru teachers and trainers over the years (especially Louise, Orina, Nigel, Ruth, Rita, Maggie and Barbara): your love, support, huge hearts and deep wisdom greatly inspire me.

To my parents, Yulan and Bob, thank you for your love and support throughout my life and for always being there in the tough times. And thank you for bringing me up to appreciate the simple and profound pleasures to be found in the abundant beauty of flowers, trees silhouetted against a late-afternoon winter sky and all of nature.

To my beloved husband Michael – my soulmate and best friend – I express the deepest gratitude from my heart and soul for your complete and utter belief in me and your unwavering support for all that I do. I would not be following my soul's path in life and this book wouldn't exist without you. I am blessed that you came into my life with your sideways lens and ca06.

And finally, thank you to you, dear reader, for being willing to dive deeply into your heart and find the peace which lies within. You light up the world.

About the Author

Stella Tomlinson is a Hampshire (UK)-based teacher, writer and energy worker empowering sensitive, soulful people to connect to inner peace by living in rhythm with the cycles and flow of life through movement, rest, meditation, guided self-enquiry, ceremony and cycle and seasonal awareness in alignment with their needs as a high sensitive.

She's been on the path of exploring the mind, body and spirit connection since 2000 at the same time as beginning her working life in the university sector where she has been an information specialist, a communications consultant, and a web editor as well as working in internal communications. She left the world of being an employee in 2016 to focus on her writing and teaching full-time.

Stella has been writing about the life-transforming effects of yoga since 2011 and began teaching Dru Yoga in 2012 after completing their two year, 200-hour training. She then completed a 2-year Dru Meditation Teacher Training 2014-16.

She teaches weekly Dru Yoga classes; a monthly meditation class; a monthly 'Essential Rest' class; and Soul Space for Sensitives events, all in the Southampton and district area. She's currently developing new in-person and online offerings which will be available from 2019.

In recent years she's become drawn to feeling and working with the subtle energies of the body through the energy block release sequences of Dru Yoga; energy healing with Jikiden Reiki; and improving emotional and energetic understanding and flow through Energy Medicine and Energy Emotional Freedom Technique of which she is now a Master Practitioner. In 2018 she began a new journey, to train to become a Priestess of Brighde-Brigantia.

Stella has been featured on BBC Radio and her writing has appeared in publications including OM Yoga magazine, Elephant Journal and Less Stress London.

When she's not teaching or writing Stella loves reading, walking in nature, hugging trees, taking pictures of the sky, gazing at flowers, listening to birdsong, moon-bathing, and exploring earth-based spirituality by living in alignment with the cycles of the moon and menstruation, and the rhythms and flow of the sun and the seasons.

stellatomlinson.com

31910615R00148

Printed in Poland
by Amazon Fulfillment
Poland Sp. z o.o., Wrocław